Keep this book. You will need it and use it throughout your career.

About the American Hotel & Lodging Association (AH&LA)

Founded in 1910, AH&LA is the trade association representing the lodging industry in the United States. AH&LA is a federation of state lodging associations throughout the United States with 11,000 lodging properties worldwide as members. The association offers its members assistance with governmental affairs representation, communications, marketing, hospitality operations, training and education, technology issues, and more. For information, call 202-289-3100.

LODGING, the management magazine of AH&LA, is a "living textbook" for hospitality students that provides timely features, industry news, and vital lodging information.

About the Educational Institute of AH&LA (EI)

An affiliate of AH&LA, the Educational Institute is the world's largest source of quality training and educational materials for the lodging industry. EI develops textbooks and courses that are used in more than 1,200 colleges and universities worldwide, and also offers courses to individuals through its Distance Learning program. Hotels worldwide rely on EI for training resources that focus on every aspect of lodging operations. Industry-tested videos, CD-ROMs, seminars, and skills guides prepare employees at every skill level. EI also offers professional certification for the industry's top performers. For information about EI's products and services, call 800-349-0299 or 407-999-8100.

About the American Hotel & Lodging Educational Foundation (AH&LEF)

An affiliate of AH&LA, the American Hotel & Lodging Educational Foundation provides financial support that enhances the stability, prosperity, and growth of the lodging industry through educational and research programs. AH&LEF has awarded hundreds of thousands of dollars in scholarship funds for students pursuing higher education in hospitality management. AH&LEF has also funded research projects on topics important to the industry, including occupational safety and health, turnover and diversity, and best practices in the U.S. lodging industry. For information, call 202-289-3180.

00885TXT01ENGE
PP-1937

ETHICS IN THE HOSPITALITY AND TOURISM INDUSTRY

Educational Institute Books

UNIFORM SYSTEM OF ACCOUNTS FOR THE LODGING
INDUSTRY
Tenth Revised Edition

RESORT DEVELOPMENT AND MANAGEMENT
Second Edition
Chuck Y. Gee

PLANNING AND CONTROL FOR FOOD AND BEVERAGE
OPERATIONS
Sixth Edition
Jack D. Ninemeier

UNDERSTANDING HOSPITALITY LAW
Fourth Edition
Jack P. Jefferies/Banks Brown

SUPERVISION IN THE HOSPITALITY INDUSTRY
Third Edition
Raphael R. Kavanaugh/Jack D. Ninemeier

MANAGEMENT OF FOOD AND BEVERAGE OPERATIONS
Fourth Edition
Jack D. Ninemeier

MANAGING FRONT OFFICE OPERATIONS
Seventh Edition
Michael L. Kasavana/Richard M. Brooks

MANAGING SERVICE IN FOOD AND BEVERAGE
OPERATIONS
Third Edition
Ronald F. Cichy/Philip J. Hickey, Jr.

THE LODGING AND FOOD SERVICE INDUSTRY
Sixth Edition
Gerald W. Lattin

SECURITY AND LOSS PREVENTION MANAGEMENT
Second Edition
Raymond C. Ellis, Jr./David M. Stipanuk

HOSPITALITY INDUSTRY MANAGERIAL ACCOUNTING
Sixth Edition
Raymond S. Schmidgall

PURCHASING FOR HOSPITALITY OPERATIONS
William B. Virts

MANAGING TECHNOLOGY IN THE HOSPITALITY
INDUSTRY
Fourth Edition
Michael L. Kasavana/John J. Cahill

BASIC HOTEL AND RESTAURANT ACCOUNTING
Sixth Edition
Raymond Cote

ACCOUNTING FOR HOSPITALITY MANAGERS
Fourth Edition
Raymond Cote

CONVENTION MANAGEMENT AND SERVICE
Seventh Edition
Milton T. Astroff/James R. Abbey

HOSPITALITY SALES AND MARKETING
Fourth Edition
James R. Abbey

MANAGING HOUSEKEEPING OPERATIONS
Second Edition
Margaret M. Kappa/Aleta Nitschke/Patricia B. Schappert

DIMENSIONS OF TOURISM
Joseph D. Fridgen

HOSPITALITY TODAY: AN INTRODUCTION
Fifth Edition
Rocco M. Angelo/Andrew N. Vladimir

MANAGING BAR AND BEVERAGE OPERATIONS
Lendal H. Kotschevar/Mary L. Tanke

ETHICS IN HOSPITALITY MANAGEMENT: A BOOK OF
READINGS
Edited by Stephen S. J. Hall

HOSPITALITY FACILITIES MANAGEMENT AND DESIGN
Third Edition
David M. Stipanuk

MANAGING HOSPITALITY HUMAN RESOURCES
Fourth Edition
Robert H. Woods

FINANCIAL MANAGEMENT FOR THE HOSPITALITY
INDUSTRY
William P. Andrew/Raymond S. Schmidgall

HOSPITALITY INDUSTRY FINANCIAL ACCOUNTING
Third Edition
Raymond S. Schmidgall/James W. Damitio

INTERNATIONAL HOTEL MANAGEMENT
Chuck Y. Gee

QUALITY SANITATION MANAGEMENT
Ronald F. Cichy

HOTEL INVESTMENTS: ISSUES & PERSPECTIVES
Fourth Edition
Edited by Lori E. Raleigh and Rachel J. Roginsky

LEADERSHIP AND MANAGEMENT IN THE HOSPITALITY
INDUSTRY
Second Edition
Robert H. Woods/Judy Z. King

MARKETING IN THE HOSPITALITY INDUSTRY
Fourth Edition
Ronald A. Nykiel

CONTEMPORARY HOSPITALITY MARKETING
William Lazer/Roger Layton

UNIFORM SYSTEM OF ACCOUNTS FOR THE HEALTH,
RACQUET AND SPORTSCLUB INDUSTRY

CONTEMPORARY CLUB MANAGEMENT
Second Edition
Edited by Joe Perdue for the Club Managers Association of America

RESORT CONDOMINIUM AND VACATION OWNERSHIP
MANAGEMENT: A HOSPITALITY PERSPECTIVE
Robert A. Gentry/Pedro Mandoki/Jack Rush

ACCOUNTING FOR CLUB OPERATIONS
Raymond S. Schmidgall/James W. Damitio

TRAINING AND DEVELOPMENT FOR THE
HOSPITALITY INDUSTRY
Debra F. Cannon/Catherine M. Gustafson

UNIFORM SYSTEM OF FINANCIAL REPORTING FOR CLUBS
Sixth Revised Edition

HOTEL ASSET MANAGEMENT: PRINCIPLES & PRACTICES
Edited by Paul Beals and Greg Denton

MANAGING BEVERAGE SERVICE
Lendal H. Kotschevar/Ronald F. Cichy

FOOD SAFETY: MANAGING THE HACCP PROCESS
Ronald F. Cichy

UNIFORM SYSTEM OF FINANCIAL REPORTING FOR SPAS

FUNDAMENTALS OF DESTINATION MANAGEMENT AND
MARKETING
Edited by Rich Harrill

ETHICS IN THE HOSPITALITY AND TOURISM INDUSTRY
Karen Lieberman/Bruce Nissen

HOSPITALITY AND TOURISM MARKETING
William Lazer/Melissa Dallas/Carl Riegel

12/06

ETHICS
IN THE
HOSPITALITY
AND TOURISM
INDUSTRY

Karen Lieberman, Ph.D.
Bruce Nissen, Ph.D.

EDUCATIONAL INSTITUTE
American Hotel & Lodging Association

Disclaimer

This publication is designed to provide accurate and authoritative information in regard to the subject matter covered. It is sold with the understanding that the publisher is not engaged in rendering legal, accounting, or other professional service. If legal advice or other expert assistance is required, the services of a competent professional person should be sought.

—*From the Declaration of Principles jointly adopted by the American Bar Association and a Committee of Publishers and Associations*

Nothing contained in this publication shall constitute a standard, an endorsement, or a recommendation of the Institute or AH&LA. The Institute and AH&LA disclaim any liability with respect to the use of any information, procedure, or product, or reliance thereon by any member of the hospitality industry.

©2005
By the EDUCATIONAL INSTITUTE of the
AMERICAN HOTEL & LODGING ASSOCIATION
2113 N. High Street
Lansing, Michigan 48906

The Educational Institute of the American
Hotel & Lodging Association is a nonprofit
educational foundation.

Printed in the United States of America
    5 6 7 8 9 09 08 07 D

ISBN 978–0–86612–275–7

DEDICATION

As always, for Leif and Jared
And now, for Heather and Annie, too

Contents

About the Authors xiii

1 Introduction 1

The Language of Ethics 1
Ethical Understanding 2

Business Ethics • Is It Enough to Obey the Law? • Is Ethical Behavior Good for Business? • Moral Responsibility • Making Ethical Decisions

Chapter Questions 15
Thinking Exercise 15

2 Utilitarianism: The Greatest Good 17

What Is the "Good?" • Jeremy Bentham: Pleasures and Pains • John Stuart Mill: The Quality of Happiness • Strong Points of Utilitarianism • A Major Criticism of Utilitarianism • Two Types of Utilitarianism • Utilitarianism: A Summary

Chapter Questions 23
Thinking Exercise 24

3 Kantian Ethics: Duties and Rights 25

It's the Motive that Counts • What Is Our Duty • Categorical Imperative: First Formulation • Categorical Imperative: Second Formulation • Strengths of Kant's System • Kant and the Concept of "Rights" • Negative Rights and Positive Rights • Applicability • Conflicting Duties • Are Consequences Irrelevant? • Libertarianism • Objections to Libertarianism • Kantian Ethics: A Summary

Chapter Questions 34
Thinking Exercise 35

4 An Ethic of Justice: Treating Others Fairly 37

Three Types of Justice • Distributive Justice • John Rawls: Justice as Fairness • The "Original Position" and the "Veil of Ignorance" • Strengths of Rawl's System • The Basic Principles of Justice • Principle of Equal Liberty • The Difference Principle • The Principle of Fair Equality of Opportunity • Criticisms of Rawls • Applying Rawls: An Illustration • Retributive Justice • Compensatory Justice

Chapter Questions 48
Thinking Exercise 48

5 Virtue Ethics: Aristotle and the Good Life **49**

> *Judging Character • Aristotle: A Virtuous Character • The Golden Mean • Virtue Examples • The Relationship of Virtues to Moral Principles • The Relationship of Virtues to "Human Nature" • Criticisms of Virtue Ethics • Virtue Ethics and Social Institutions*

Chapter Questions 54
Thinking Exercise 54

6 Applying Ethics to the Purchasing, Marketing and Sales Functions **55**

Case Study—A Trip to Las Vegas 56
Case Commentary: Utilitarianism 57
Case Commentary: Kant's Categorical Imperative 58
Case Commentary: The Ethic of Justice 60
Case Commentary: Aristotle and the Ethics of Virtue 61
Conclusion 62
Case Study—Spilled Coffee 63
Case Study—The Board of Directors 64
Case Study—The Ride to Paradise 65
Case Study—The Head Shipper 66
Case Study—Theresa the Telemarketer 67

7 Applying Ethics to the Maintenance and Housekeeping Functions **71**

Case Study—On the Edge 72
Case Commentary: Utilitarianism 74
Case Commentary: Kant's Categorical Imperative 74
Case Commentary: The Ethic of Justice 75
Case Commentary: Aristotle and the Ethics of Virtue 76
Case Study—The VIP 77
Case Study—The Housekeeper's Paycheck 78
Case Study—Dissatisfaction 80
Case Study—Only Your Housekeeper Knows for Sure 82
Case Study—The Renovation 82

8 Applying Ethics to the Food and Beverage Function **85**

Case Study—A Good Job Pays Your Bills 86
Case Commentary: Utilitarianism 87
Case Commentary: Kant's Categorical Imperative 87
Case Commentary: The Ethic of Justice 88

Case Commentary: Aristotle and the Ethics of Virtue 89
Case Study—Sound Business Practices 90
Case Study—Stolen Lobster Tails 91
Case Study—To Drive or Not to Drive? 92
Case Study—Clean as a Whistle! 93
Case Study—Ratting 94
Case Study—Tip Reporting 94
Case Study—Your Heart's Delight 95
Case Study—Something for Nothing 95

9   Applying Ethics to the Hotel Front Office Function **97**

Case Study—Things Go Bump in the Night 97
Case Commentary: Utilitarianism 98
Case Commentary: Kant's Categorical Imperative 99
Case Commentary: The Ethic of Justice 100
Case Commentary: Aristotle and the Ethics of Virtue 101
Case Study—The Wedding Party 101
Case Study—Nobody Will Ever Know 102
Case Study—Front Desk Politics 103
Case Study—Always Read the Small Print 104
Case Study—The Safety Sheet 105
Case Study—Who Are You Anyway? 105
Case Study—Blowing the Whistle 106
Case Study—Lady of the Night 106
Case Study—"But What Happened to My Room?" 107

10   Ethics and the Human Resources Management Function **109**

Case Study—Salary Disclosure 109
Case Commentary: Utilitarianism 110
Case Commentary: Kant's Categorical Imperative 111
Case Commentary: The Ethic of Justice 112
Case Commentary: Aristotle and the Ethics of Virtue 113
Case Study—Discriminating Forces 113
Case Study—The Come On 115
Case Study—Is this Sexual Harassment? 116
Case Study—Taking Credit 117
Case Study—Stars Are Difficult to Come By 119
Case Study—Blue Vest Pizza and Customer Satisfaction 120
Case Study—But Can She Do the Job? 122

**11 Applying Ethics to Maintain an Environmentally
Sound Hospitality and Tourism Industry** **125**

Case Study—Gray Water/Black Water Overflow 126
Case Commentary: The Company 130
Case Commentary: The Individuals 131
Case Study—All Roads Lead to the Resort 133
Case Study—It's No Big Deal 135
Case Study—Safety First 136

**12 Ethics and Public Policy in the Hospitality
and Tourism Industry** **139**

Case Study—The Public Exposure Debate 141
Case Commentary 144
Case Study—A Fair Price to Pay 146
Case Study—Second-Hand Rose 147
Case Study—Fishy Facts: The Good, the Bad, and the Ugly 148
Case Study—Loyal Beyond the Letter of the Law 149
Case Study—Menu Management 149

Index **151**

About the Authors

Karen Lieberman is Professor and Chair of the Hospitality College, Johnson & Wales University, Florida campus, North Miami, Florida. She was previously Department Chair and Associate Professor, Purdue University North Central, Westville, Indiana. She holds a B.A. degree from New York University (Near Eastern Languages & Literature), a master's degree from Purdue University (Restaurant, Hotel, Institutional Management and Nutrition) and a Ph.D. from Purdue University (Educational Administration). She is also a Registered Dietitian.

Dr. Lieberman is the author of "Nutrition and Disease" (Garland Publishers), as well as many scholarly articles. In 2003, she was awarded an Emerald Management Review Citation of Excellence. She has been an active member of CHRIE since 1988 and has served on several committees, and as President of Florida/Caribbean CHRIE. She serves on many civic and community boards in the Miami area.

Bruce Nissen is the Director of Research at the Center for Labor Research and Studies at Florida International University (FIU) in Miami, Florida. He also directs FIU's Research Institute on Social and Economic Policy (RISEP). He holds a B.A. degree from Grinnell College and a Ph.D. in Philosophy (Ethics) from Columbia University.

Dr. Nissen has previously authored or edited seven scholarly books, and is also the author of numerous academic journal articles and book chapters. In 2004, he was awarded FIU's university-wide Excellence in Research award. Dr. Nissen is widely quoted in regional and national media, and has served on boards and commissions of both community organizations and government agencies.

Dr. Lieberman and Dr. Nissen are husband and wife. They are the parents of two grown sons, Leif and Jared. "Ethics in the Hospitality and Tourism Industry" is their first book together, although they often present workshops and seminars together on the topic of hospitality ethics.

(Photo of Drs. Lieberman and Nissen by Barry Greff.)

1

Introduction

UNLIKE THE WORLD OF FACTS which is concerned with "what is," ethics is concerned with "what ought to be." Ethics is the study of moral principles concerning "rightful" conduct based on our most deeply held values. This book focuses on a particular branch of ethics, business ethics, and, more particularly, ethics within a particular branch of business—the hospitality and tourism industry. We will examine ethical issues that apply to individuals working in the industry and to organizations whose norms and internal cultures encourage ethical or unethical behavior.

The Language of Ethics

Throughout this book, the terms "ethics" and "morality" are used interchangeably. What is ethical is considered moral; what is unethical is considered immoral. Ethical discussions focus on the "right thing to do" or the "wrong thing to do." When used in this way, "right" and "wrong" are ethical terms. However, "right" and "wrong" are not always used in the ethical sense. For example, we could say that the right way to play golf is with a certain kind of swing that hits the ball straight, while the wrong way to play is with a swing that hits the ball so it curves off the fairway. There is no ethical or moral dimension to how we hit a golf ball, but there is when we discuss whether cheating on your golf score is right or wrong.

Other terms that we often use when we think about ethics or morality are "good" and "evil," especially when we use these terms as opposites. We also speak of "moral obligations" or "moral responsibilities" when we refer to what a person or organization ought to do. Sometimes, we say that it is a person's "duty" to behave in a certain way, or that they "should" behave in a certain way. When we do, we are making a moral or ethical judgment, either about that person's character or about that person's actions. Not all judgments are ethical judgments. For example, it is not an ethical judgment when we judge the color of a restaurant menu as attractive or unattractive.

Another ethical norm that we frequently appeal to is "fairness." If we say that something is not fair, that statement is an ethical or moral judgment. Closely related is the standard of "justice." We want our society and our institutions to be just, and that too is an ethical judgment. Another ethical standard we employ is that of "rights," as when we say that someone's rights were violated and this is wrong and immoral. For example, consider a restaurant chain in which managers and franchisees conspire to limit the number of black employees and to restrict those employed to menial tasks. If a restaurant company engages in practices like

1

these, it is not acting in a fair, moral, or just way towards its employees—their rights are being violated.

Ethical norms differ from other norms or rules in that they are not the result of government legislation or some organizational rule-setting process. They are not the same as laws (although hopefully there is a considerable overlap). Something could be perfectly legal yet immoral. For example, slavery is an immoral institution, but it was legal in the United States for a long time. As late as the 1960s, black people were not permitted to eat with whites in many restaurants. Separate facilities existed for white and black people, and blacks were only allowed to sit in the rear of buses. This was all perfectly legal in parts of the United States—but was it moral?

So what exactly puts something in the "moral" or "ethical" category? Ethical or moral norms concern our most deeply held values, the things we most cherish and the things we most despise. As such, they concern actions that we believe either greatly benefit or greatly injure human beings. We believe that ethical or moral norms are more important than other values, such as our own self-interest or material comfort. If there is a conflict between "doing the right thing" and doing something that is wrong, but makes us wealthier, or more comfortable—we should do the ethical thing. For example, if our menu says fresh fish, we should serve fresh fish—even if frozen fish could be offered at a much lower cost to the restaurant.

Ethical Understanding

Some believe that ethics is not something you can teach others, nor is it something that you "learn." According to this view, people either have it, or they do not. It is certainly true that moral reasoning begins in childhood, and that an upbringing that guides a young person toward ethical behavior is critical to an ethical understanding. A young adult who has not consistently been taught right from wrong will more likely go astray than those who have had a consistent ethical viewpoint given to them from childhood.

However, this does not mean that adults cannot learn and change in this area. Adults are able to change their views, and even more important, to deepen their understanding of ethical or moral issues. The field of social psychology has shown that adults can grow and change in their moral sensitivity and reasoning just as they can in other areas. At the very least, simply subjecting your moral beliefs and intuitions to a systematic look cannot be a bad thing—it can only help you think through the issues more clearly.

A closely related objection is the view that ethics cannot be taught because morality is a private affair. You cannot teach someone ethics any more than you can teach them that something tastes good or bad. Morality is specific to an individual; what is right for me may be wrong for you, and vice versa. Therefore, there is no point in studying ethics because you cannot tell someone what their private belief system should be.

This view may hold in some situations in which no large moral principles are involved. It might be true, for example, that it is right for me to donate to a certain charity but wrong for you do so because I can afford it but, if you do, your family will suffer. In this case, what is "right" and what is "wrong" for each of us depends a lot on our individual circumstances, and the right choice will depend on many factors that have to be considered. The "right" thing and the "wrong" thing can depend a lot on circumstances. Imagine two hotels, one very large with many conference rooms; the other relatively small with only one conference room. The large hotel donates a conference room to a scout troop once a month. When a second scout troop approaches the smaller hotel, the owner has to deny the scouts because the only conference room must be available for business purposes.

Does this mean, however, that right and wrong, moral and immoral, have no real grounding? Is it up to each individual to decide his or her own moral beliefs any way he or she wishes, with no need to justify the choices? Can it really be true that any set of ethical or moral beliefs is as good as another? If that were true, a person who engaged in murder or rape and who thought this was perfectly okay would be just as moral as one who treated others with respect and compassion. Is it really true that someone who believes that Adolf Hitler's genocide of millions of people is morally acceptable is on just as solid moral standing as all of the rest of the world, which universally condemns the Holocaust as evil?

By its very nature, ethics or morality cannot be a purely private affair because moral principles are intended to guide our conduct in relationships with each other. We may not reach agreement on ethical or moral principles as easily as we can on "matters of fact," but this does not mean there is no basis for justifying or refuting one's moral or ethical judgments.

It is striking that, with all their differences, the major moral and ethical systems of the world, along with virtually all of the world's great religions, have an enormous overlap in what they condone and condemn. None of them condone, as a matter of principle, murder, rape, genocide, intentional cruelty to other human beings, etc. While delusional or fanatical individuals (whose factual belief systems are also warped beyond recognition) attempt to use a great moral or religious belief system to justify such actions, they simply misinterpret and misapply the belief system. In fact, there is a fairly large convergence among the great ethical and moral theories, which is encouraging evidence that morality or ethics is not merely a matter of individual taste requiring no further justification. We can, and should, justify and defend our ethical beliefs and examine them for indefensible assumptions or reasoning so that we can more intelligently lead an ethical life.

Business Ethics

Even if we grant that ethics is an important area of study and reflection for individuals, some have argued that there is no basis for applying ethics to the world of business. According to this way of thinking, the two do not mix. The cynical view sees business operations as inherently corrupt and beyond redemption. In an era where the news headlines frequently feature corporations that have employed "off-the-balance-sheet," fake subsidiaries to deceive investors, accounting firms that hide financial irregularities, companies that rip off taxpayers by overcharging the government or charging for services never performed, senior managers who enrich themselves while they bankrupt their companies and impoverish their workers, inside traders who become multimillionaires through buying and selling stock on the basis of information kept from ordinary investors, companies apparently "buying" legislation through donations to public officials, whistleblowers being treated badly instead of the wrongdoers they expose—it is easy to be cynical.

The hospitality industry is no different. Victor Posner, owner of DWG Corporation, which owns Arby's, was known for improperly enriching himself by running public companies as private preserves. Even after he was caught, it was found that DWG was using company money to clean his private home and do his laundry.[1]

However, cynicism provides nothing constructive to the moral dilemmas we face. In fact, it feeds into the very problems to which it responds. The more cynical people become, the more open the atmosphere to ethical improprieties, which then become a "way of life." A vicious circle sets in, and unethical practices and cynicism mutually reinforce each other. The most cynical societies are those that are the most corrupt. There are both practical and ethical reasons why cynicism is not a productive response to the unethical practices you may see in the world around you. A much more useful response is to do what you can to see that practices that poison the business atmosphere are changed.

A much different argument is that business executives and managers have few, if any, ethical obligations to anyone other than their owners. Therefore "business ethics" is a lot of mumbo-jumbo, imposing inappropriate standards on businesses. The best-known exponent of this view is Milton Friedman, the conservative economist who is widely recognized for arguing that businesses have essentially no obligations other than to maximize profits for their owners or shareholders. Friedman has argued that the only ethical responsibility of the corporate executive is to the company's owners. That responsibility is to "make as much money as possible while conforming to the basic rules of the society, both those embodied in law and those embodied in ethical custom."[2] Friedman also maintains that the only social responsibility is profit maximization, as long as you stay within the rules of the game, meaning that you compete openly without fraud and deception.

Friedman's argument is an interesting ethical one, but it does not avoid ethical questions. Instead, it strongly asserts one particular ethical viewpoint, the viewpoint that the single-minded pursuit of profit will result in the most ethically advantageous situation for all concerned. This may or may not be true, but it is an ethical assertion in either case. A number of writers have questioned Friedman's belief that pure selfishness of each leads to the best possible outcome for all. Even Friedman argues that business leaders, in addition to maximizing profits, must (1) obey the law, and (2) follow ethical custom. We will deal with the relationship between morality and the law later. The addition of "ethical custom" could add a large number of responsibilities onto businesses. For example, does ethical custom

---

[1] Steve Brooks, "At the Trials of Chairman Posner," *Restaurant Business,* vol 91 (May 20, 1992), pg. 88.

[2] Milton Friedman, "The Social Responsibility of Business is to Increase Its Profits," *The New York Times,* September 13, 1970. Reprinted in Shari Collins-Chobanian, ed., *Ethical Challenges to Business as Usual* (Upper Saddle River, N.J.: Pearson/Prentice Hall, 2004), pp. 224–229.

require that companies adhere to any standards regarding a fair compensation of employees? Milton Friedman apparently wants ethical custom to mean very little, and he never refers to any business obligations that arise out of extra-legal ethical concerns again in his article. However, he does acknowledge that they exist, and we need to explore what those obligations are if we wish to arrive at acceptable standards for business conduct.

Another view that attempts to absolve business leaders and personnel from ethical obligations beyond maximizing profits is what Alex Michales has called the "loyal agent's argument."[3] The argument is that a manager has to be a loyal agent of his or her employer, and therefore has a duty to serve the employer. The employer would like to have his or her self-interest served, and therefore the manager (and presumably other employees as well) has a duty to serve the self-interest of the employer in any manner that will further that self-interest.

There are a number of problems with this argument. It assumes that the "loyal agent" duty is the only duty of a manager or employee. Are there no limits to this duty? Are there no other duties? Are there no other "stakeholders" to whom you have any obligations, beyond the shareholders or owners of the company?

The "loyal agent" argument is morally suspect because it attempts to exempt a person from moral responsibility for his or her actions by hiding behind an organizational barrier. If there is no moral responsibility of individuals running an organization, and if by their very nature "organizations" are hard to hold morally accountable, this begins to look like an attempt to evade all moral responsibilities altogether. Particularly in the field of business ethics, where the temptation to "cut moral corners" for the sake of self-gain is great, it is important to be on the lookout for arguments that are simply rationalizations of self-interest that avoid normal ethical responsibilities.

Consider the following loyal agent example within the hospitality and tourism industry. Imagine that you sell tickets for the Daytimer's Cruise Line, owned by Jay McGill. Mr. McGill tells you that he needs money to make improvements on his boat. He orders you to charge 8% tax on all tickets, instead of the required 4%. If anyone questions this practice, he wants you to tell them that it's a special tourism tax. Mr. McGill plans to use the extra 4% for his boat improvements. By agreeing to the deception, you have become a "loyal agent." Is the deception ethical because you are loyally acting as the owner's agent?

Is It Enough to Obey the Law?

Some argue that the only ethical or moral norm a business needs to follow is to obey the law. As long as it is not illegal, it is okay. This is a fairly widespread attitude, but it runs into some real problems if you take it seriously. Equating the law and morality can lead to perspectives that do not seem to square with our ethical views. First, as we have already noted, there are times and places where the law has condoned and even required immoral behavior. The pre–Civil War laws in

---

3 See Alex C. Michales, *A Pragmatic Approach to Business Ethics* (Thousand Oaks, Calif.: Sage Publications, 1995).

the south of the United States upheld slavery, and required people to turn in runaway slaves. We now know that this was absolutely immoral. In Nazi Germany, anti-Semitic behavior was required, and some non-Jewish Germans were even put to death for speaking out against the Nazi atrocities or for attempting to protect the Jewish population from slaughter. As recently as forty-five years ago, the so-called "Jim Crow" laws in the southern United States required racial discrimination, and a black man would sometimes be lynched for simply looking at a white woman or for failing to show a submissive enough attitude toward white people in the street. Even in a democracy, laws can occasionally get off the track morally.

Beyond the extreme examples cited above, legality cannot be equated with morality because many of our laws have little to do with morality. They are actually conventions, or rules, that make our lives more orderly or convenient, but they lack any important moral content. A good example would be the parking laws of a city. There is nothing distinctively moral about this form of regulation, but it does make our lives more orderly. A code regulating upkeep of front yards is a further example. A law declaring a certain day to be a national holiday is another. While all of these may be considered "moral" issues in the same extended sense that almost everything one does as a human being may have some remote moral consequence, in general, these matters are not considered moral ones, but rather matters of convenience. Just like good manners or proper etiquette are perhaps not serious enough matters to be considered deeply moral, the same is true for many laws.

Equating legality with morality is also faulty because something may be legal but immoral. For example, there is nothing in the law in the United States preventing an employer from firing an employee for no reason whatsoever who has faithfully and loyally done a good job for fifteen years. You can fire an employee simply because you found out this morning that he is a cousin to somebody you detest. You can fire people because their new contact lenses make their eyes look brown, and you do not like brown eyes. This freedom to fire is known as the legal "employment-at-will" doctrine; only certain types of hiring and firing discrimination (on the basis of race, gender, skin color, national origin, handicap, etc.) are illegal. Consider the front desk agent who has been a loyal employee for many years. A new general manager would like a job for his nephew. There is nothing in the law preventing the manager from hiring his nephew and firing the long-term employee.

Legal though it may be, the morality of firing a good, long-term loyal employee for no reason whatsoever (or for a reason that has nothing to do with his or her job performance) is highly questionable. We would say that such a firing, although legal, is unethical or immoral. Similarly, if for some bizarre reason an employer decided in times of layoff to terminate the most needy employees with the largest families first, we would find this to be contrary to our ethical or moral standards, even though it is perfectly legal, absent a union contract or a written policy stating that layoffs will be in order of seniority or some other more rational criteria.

While legality and morality are not identical, there is obviously a large overlap. A good number of our more strongly held moral beliefs are written into law, making their violation a transgression of both our moral standards and the law.

Laws everywhere make a number of immoral actions illegal, including murder, rape, assault, theft, fraud, etc. While some unethical practices and forms of behavior are illegal, not all are, and the law probably cannot be made so detailed that it makes all immoral practices illegal.

Is Ethical Behavior Good for Business?

The distinction between legal and ethical standards suggests the need to categorize different realms of business activity. A useful set of categories for the responsibilities of businesses has been developed by Archie B. Carroll.[4] Two categories are fairly obvious and widely recognized: *economic responsibilities*, whereby the business must achieve satisfactory financial results (for example, make a profit), and *legal responsibilities*, whereby the business must abide by the nation's laws and regulations (for example, pay taxes). *Discretionary responsibilities* are responsibilities that a company may elect in order to meet the expectations of some of its customers or a particular element in society. An example would be philanthropic activities, whereby a company chooses to give to the arts or to donate to certain charities in the local community. A good example of this is the Ronald McDonald House. Beyond these three categories are *ethical responsibilities*, whereby society expects compliance with norms of behavior that may not be written into law but are, nevertheless, necessary for the business to operate properly.

It can be argued that well-managed businesses meet or exceed expectations at economic, legal, and ethical levels. However, there is much debate about whether there might be a conflict of interest between doing well in one area and doing well in another. Some writers stress the potential conflict between the need to do well economically and doing well ethically (or sometimes, even legally). Supporting this view are well known cases such as Enron, which made itself one of the most economically successful businesses in the United States (at least temporarily) powering a phenomenal ride to the top by massive fraud and other unethical practices. Adelphia, WorldCom, and other businesses that were spectacularly successful economically, until caught in unethical and probably illegal behavior, add further support. A well-known case in hospitality and tourism involved the 2002 Winter Olympics. In their successful bid to host the winter games, Salt Lake City employees bribed members of the Olympic officials with cash and benefits amounting to almost $800,000. After the scandal broke, their defense was that they were "playing by the unwritten rules" for Olympic site selection.[5]

All too often, we see companies and individuals making a lot of money by engaging in practices that seem to contradict our ethical beliefs. We need to ask if being ethical is "good business." Does an ethical approach to business lead to

---

[4] The following categories are taken from the work of Archie B. Carroll. See Archie B. Carroll, "A Three Dimensional Conceptual Model of Corporate Performance," *Academy of Management Review*, 4, (1979), 497–505. See also Archie B. Carroll, "The Pyramid of Corporate Social Responsibility: Toward the Moral Management of Organizational Stakeholders," *Business Horizons*, 34 (4), (1991), 39–48.

[5] *Economist*, Jan 30, 1999, pp. 42

financial success? Those who have looked at this question do not have a definitive answer.

We know that most businesses must abide by at least some minimal legal and ethical standards or we could not conduct business with each other. If all companies routinely lied, cheated, and deceived commerce would grind to a halt. No one would trust anyone: promises would not be kept; checks would not be accepted. Billing would be impossible because invoices would likely not be paid. Banking would be impossible, because bank officials would likely run off with customers' deposits. Loans would never be made, and so on. All transactions would have to occur instantaneously, with cash changing hands at exactly the same time that goods or services are delivered.

Therefore, businesses have to abide by certain basic rules of conduct if the system of business is to work at all. Underlying those basic rules of conduct are ethical practices regarding honesty, respect for other human beings, and the like. So, a case can obviously be made that at least minimal standards of ethical behavior are built into the very business practices of a market system.

The difficult question is whether individual businesses (hotels, restaurants, airlines, etc.) or businesspersons can serve their own self-interests best by breaking some of those rules and violating accepted ethical standards. If it is a legal matter, and there are substantial penalties for breaking the law, companies and individuals will not be serving their best self-interest in the long run if they are caught because they will end up in jail and/or with stiff fines. But what if they do not get caught? Or, what if the law has such weak penalties that even if they do get caught, they come out ahead financially and do not go to jail? Even beyond the law, what if they can make substantial sums of money by engaging in deceptive or abusive practices that are not illegal?

In important ways, these questions address the relationship between our individual self-interest and our collective self-interest. The problematic nature of this relationship is posed by philosophers through a puzzle called the "prisoner's dilemma."[6] While there are a number of ways to illustrate the prisoner's dilemma issue, a standard example is as follows:

> *Two men are arrested for committing a crime. Secretly, they promise each other that each will both deny having committed the crime. The police department separates the two prisoners, and tells them both the same thing. If both men deny having committed the crime, they each will get one year in prison. If both confess, they each will get two years in prison. However, if one confesses while the other denies committing the crime, the person who confesses will be freed but the other will get three years in prison.*

---

[6] For more on the "prisoner's dilemma" problem, see Anatol Rapaport and A. Chammah, *The Prisoner's Dilemma* (Ann Arbor, Mich.: University of Michigan Press, 1965). For a view of the large volume of research that has been done on the prisoner's dilemma, see William Poundstone, *Prisoner's Dilemma* (New York: Doubleday, 1992).

Exhibit 1   Outcomes in the Prisoner's Dilemma Situation

	Other Prisoner denies	Other prisoner confesses
You deny	**You get one year in jail** Other prisoner gets one year in jail	**You get three years in jail** Other prisoner goes free
You confess	**You go free** Other prisoner get three years in jail	**You get two years in jail** Other prisoner gets two years in jail

If you were one of the prisoners, what would you do? For the purposes of this exercise, put aside any feelings you might have for the other prisoner. You are only to think of your own self-interest; you are to do only what is best for yourself. What would you do? Economic theory for a market system like capitalism assumes that companies and individuals act rationally and strictly in their own self-interest. This theory assumes that all economic or business transactions are carried out for reasons of self-interest—not because we like each other or want to help each other. A for-profit restaurant or hotel, for example, serves its customers with the goal of making a profit, not because it "likes" those customers and wants to give them a gift or do them a favor.

For the purpose of working through the prisoner's dilemma, assume the same attitude. Think through the situation rationally; do what is in your own self-interest. Would you stick to your promise, cooperate with the other prisoner, and deny having committed the crime? Or, would you break the promise to the other prisoner, betray your fellow prisoner, and confess to the crime? To help you think through the alternatives, Exhibit 1 shows the outcomes of each possible decision.

Notice the outcomes for you (printed in bold in Exhibit 1) if you keep your promise and deny committing the crime. In that case, you will get either one year in jail or three years in jail, depending on what the other prisoner does. Notice the outcomes if you break your promise and confess to the crime. You will either go free or get two years in jail. In both sets of outcomes, you are better off breaking your promise, betraying the other prisoner, and confessing to the crime. This holds true no matter what the other prisoner does. You will be worse off, of course, if the other prisoner betrays you and confesses—in that case you both get two years in jail. Two years jail time beats three, and those are your only two alternatives if the other prisoner betrays you.

Notice that collectively your interests and those of the other prisoner are best served if you both keep your promise to each other and deny having committed the crime. In that case, the collective jail time is 2 years. If just one of you breaks the promise, the collective jail time goes up to 3 years; if both of you break the promise, the collective jail time goes up to 4 years. But the picture changes considerably if you look only at your individual self-interest. From that viewpoint, if you are going to act rationally, you should break the promise and confess.

The prisoner's dilemma is a classic situation where self-interest seems to contradict the collective, or general, interest. If you think about it, we encounter dilemmas similar to the prisoner's dilemma all the time. In general, we would all be better off if everyone followed ethical principles (do not cheat, do not lie, do not steal, do not take advantage of others when the opportunity arises, etc.). However, numerous occasions arise when we can benefit or enrich ourselves if we break those principles while, at the same time, expecting others to adhere to them. Is the prisoner's dilemma example telling us that a rational, self-interested individual should behave unethically in business whenever he or she gains from the behavior?

Perhaps that is not the proper conclusion to draw from this exercise. In most situations, we deal with others (people or businesses) on a repeated basis. Therefore, there are usually additional consequences, beyond the most immediate one, of our actions. If, in fact, unethical behavior causes your restaurant to lose "repeat customers," or causes suppliers, employees, or lending institutions to shun or sabotage your business because of its bad reputation, even your narrow individual self-interest might very well be best served by your behaving in a more ethical manner.

There is a lot of general evidence showing that reputation and trust count for a lot in most business situations.[7] Treviño and Nelson state it succinctly; "Trust is essential in a service economy where all a firm has is its reputation for dependability and good service."[8] In the case of customers, this is almost so obvious that it hardly bears repeating. Customers who feel "ripped off" by a company will very likely avoid doing business with that company in the future. Other "stakeholders" can also damage a business when they perceive that business to be unjust or immoral. Employees, for example, who believe that their employer engages in unjust decision making may retaliate through lower productivity, higher absenteeism, higher tardiness and turnover, and demands for higher wages.[9] While there is less research into the behavior of creditors or suppliers, it makes intuitive sense that they too will avoid dealing with a company that they consider to be unethical. Trust is perhaps an underrated ingredient in business relationships. A business that is unable to establish a strong sense of trust with customers, employees, and others faces a large number of obstacles to financial success. Companies that rely on repeat customers and a stable staff will find it important to establish the greatest degree of trust with them as possible.

---

[7] For a good summary of the research backing up this statement, see Manuel Velasquez, "Why Ethics Matters: A Defense of Ethics in Business Organizations," *Business Ethics Quarterly 6*, no. 2 (1996): 201–222.

[8] Linda K. Treviño and Katherine A. Nelson, *Managing Business Ethics: Straight Talk About How to Do It Right*, 3d ed. (Hoboken, N.J.: Wiley, 2004), p. 43

[9] For some of the research backing up this statement, see Robert H. Frank, "Can Socially Responsible Firms Survive in a Competitive Environment?" in David M. Messick and Ann E. Tenbrunsel, eds., *Research on Negotiations in Organizations* (Greenwich, Conn.: JAI Press, 1997). See also Robert H. Frank, *What Price the Moral High Ground? Ethical Dilemmas in Competitive Environments* (Princeton, N.J.: Princeton University Press, 2003).

Moving beyond relationships with customers, employees, creditors, and suppliers, it would seem that companies that are perceived as socially responsible are rewarded by investors, and those perceived as socially irresponsible are punished. A number of studies address corporate social responsibility and its relation to financial performance or performance on the stock market and they reach mixed results.[10] While the largest number of studies finds a positive correlation between socially responsive behavior and enhanced financial or stock performance, others find no impact at all. A few studies even find a negative relationship between social responsibility and financial success.

From all of these studies, the most one could say is that a number of them show a correlation between high profitability and socially responsible behavior. We must be careful in concluding that high ethical and "social responsibility" standards inevitably, or consistently, lead to higher profitability. The line of causality could run either way, or perhaps some third factor we have not considered leads to both high profitability and high ethical and socially responsible behavior.

Ethical behavior does not always lead to higher profits in the short run and, in some cases, perhaps not even in the long run. In our view, it depends a great deal upon whether a particular business relies on repeat customers or continuous relationships with other elements in the productive business cycle. Some businesses, including some in the hospitality industry, may be able to do just fine financially without relying on repeat customers or other ongoing relationships. If that is the case, perhaps unethical "rip-off" relationships will lead to the highest profitability. For example, let's assume that the Broadway Restaurant offers all show-goers a discount coupon in their playbill for twenty percent off their dinner entrées. However, when guests show their coupons, they are handed over-priced menus. All prices are inflated by thirty percent, giving the owners a hefty profit. The restaurant might be able to sustain this marketing and pricing strategy if the vast majority of show-goers are out-of-towners.

Most hospitality businesses rely on repeat business and word-of-mouth recommendations to be profitable. While this provides financial support for ethical behavior, a more productive view would be to discourage thinking about ethics solely in the context of financial success. If the only reason to be moral is that it "pays off" financially, people will abandon ethical behavior when it becomes apparent that more money can be made by the unethical route. We want to encourage the view that ethical accounting is a separate endeavor from financial accounting. Ethics is a sphere separate from finance, and it should be taken very seriously—not

---

[10] For one overview of these studies, see Joshua Daniel Margolis and James Patrick Walsh, *People and Profits? The Search for a Link Between a Company's Social and Financial Performance*. Mahwah, N.J.: Erlbaum, 2001). An older review of previous studies, plus a new study finding no impact one way or another is Kenneth E. Alpperle, Archie B. Carroll, and John D. Hatfield, "An Empirical Examination of the Relationship Between Corporate Social Responsibility and Profitability," *Academy of Management Journal* 28 (June 1985): pp. 449–461. A positive correlation is found in Jean B. McGuire, Alison Sundgren, and Thomas Schneeweis, "Corporate Social Responsibility and Firm Financial Performance," *Academy of Management Journal* 31 (December 1988): pp. 854–872.

just because it might lead to greater profitability, but because ethical behavior is important in its own right.

Moral Responsibility

In the event of unethical behavior, who is to blame? Are superiors to be held responsible for the unethical behavior of their subordinates? Are subordinates to be held responsible for carrying out unethical orders from their superiors? Are you responsible even if you can't do anything to prevent the unethical behavior? What if you weren't even aware of the unethical behavior? Is ignorance a defense against responsibility?

It would seem that you are not responsible for a morally reprehensible action if you are unaware of it. You should not be held responsible for something you do not know about. For example, if a restaurant cashier steals, and does an excellent job of covering up, the dining room manager might not be held responsible for the theft. However, there are limits to a defense of ignorance. If you deliberately keep yourself ignorant of something in order to avoid responsibility, you are not blameless. Consider the corporate executive who instructs underlings to not tell him about the results of studies that reveal damaging health effects of the corporation's product. He doesn't want to know because he doesn't want to be liable if the product turns out to be unsafe. Or, consider the restaurant owner who doesn't want to know about the "catch-of-the-day." Does it come from reliable sources where the waters are inspected and verified as safe, or is the catch made by local fishermen in unsafe waters? Deliberate ignorance with the intent to avoid responsibility excuses no one. Additionally, carelessness about keeping yourself reasonably informed about the consequences of your (or your company's) products or actions is also blameworthy. The degree of responsibility would probably depend on the degree of carelessness; extreme carelessness has no excuse at all.

The inability to do anything about an unethical situation could absolve one of responsibility for some morally unacceptable actions. We cannot be made responsible for something over which we have no control. In each situation, of course, there may be a dispute about whether the person could have done anything about the unethical action. Inability has to be proved; not simply asserted. A good example of this would be overcharging hotel guests. Consider a front desk agent who was fully aware that a guest had been overcharged but did nothing to correct it. The agent later claims he or she was unable to make amends. The claim might cite computer program restrictions, or company policy, or a supervisor's strict instructions. Whatever the claim, it would have to be verified before we could find the front desk agent blameless.

There are also circumstances that might lessen our responsibility. We call these "mitigating circumstances." An example would be a situation in which we are unclear or uncertain about the effects of our action, and this uncertainty is at least somewhat reasonable. Another would be a situation in which it is difficult, but not impossible, to do something to correct a morally suspect activity. A third would be a situation where the individual's involvement was minimal, or was far removed from the center of the wrongdoing. In all of these cases, we would say that the person is not blameless, but their responsibility is diminished compared to what it would be without the mitigating circumstances.

Within business organizations, assigning moral responsibility for actions becomes complicated by the chain of command. How much blame does a subordinate bear if he or she carries out clearly unethical practices, but does so under the orders of a superior? Is the excuse, "I was only following orders!" a sufficient defense of such behavior?

Imagine that Jane works for Vacationesque, a company that sells timeshares by telephone. Jane's boss, Harvey, instructs her to claim that all vacations are in four-star hotels, when the hotels are really all three-star properties. If the company is legally cited, can Jane claim, "I was only following orders" as her defense?

At best, the argument "I was only following orders" might be a mitigating circumstance. However, the claim cannot absolve you entirely of responsibility for carrying out something that you clearly knew to be immoral. The severity of the moral infraction increases as the degree to which the claim operates as a legitimate mitigating circumstance diminishes. As Manuel Velasquez puts it:

> Moral responsibility requires merely that one act freely and knowingly, and it is irrelevant that one's wrongful act is that of freely and knowingly choosing to follow an order. For example, if I am ordered by my superior to murder a competitor and I do so, I can hardly later claim that I am totally innocent because I was merely "following orders." The fact that my superior ordered me to perform what I knew was an immoral act in no way alters the fact that in performing that act I knew what I was doing and I freely chose to do it anyway and so I am morally responsible for it.[11]

While subordinates do not escape moral responsibility for their behavior simply because they are within a chain of command, it is clear that the larger responsibility falls on decision-makers. For example, a housekeeper does not escape moral responsibility when knowingly stocking guestrooms with shampoo purporting to be a name brand product that actually is a falsely labeled cheaper product. However, greater moral responsibility for this act of deception resides with the corporate manager who decided to implement the practice throughout the chain's many hotels to achieve a higher profit.

Making Ethical Decisions

What is the basis upon which we make moral or ethical decisions? Many would answer, "The values and rules I was taught as a child." That may or may not be a good basis for moral decision-making. It would depend entirely on the moral understanding of whoever taught you as a child. For some, doing as they were taught as children could mean repeating the moral lapses and mistakes of the adults who taught them. While it may be a good bet that one's parents and other caregivers had good moral values, it is wise to examine for yourself what you believe.

---

11 Manuel Velasquez, *Business Ethics: Concepts and Cases* (Upper Saddle River, N.J.: Prentice Hall, 2002), p. 54.

Unthinking adherence to someone else's rules is not a smart strategy for living your life. We do, and should, use our moral upbringing as a standard to measure the morality of different actions, but we should not simply leave it at that.

Religion and religious beliefs are another basis for making moral or ethical decisions. The world's major religions have a strong moral or ethical core to them and undoubtedly provide guidance for moral conduct. But this does not automatically resolve all ethical dilemmas. For example, religious teachings can often be applied in many ways, so simple adherence to a religious belief or religious institution may not give absolute answers to all moral questions. Many religions have multiple denominations or branches because of differences over how a commonly followed sacred text is to be understood. A number of the differences between branches or denominations of a particular religious tradition may concern weighty moral issues, such as the morality of war, what constitutes justice for the less fortunate, the morality of abortion, and the like. So, even if you follow the teachings of a particular religion, you still must determine how to follow it, and what its teachings really mean in your life. If you do this, you will inevitably be undertaking moral reflection, and you will be thinking carefully about the moral basis for your life. Thus, simply being a devout member of a certain religious tradition does not absolve you of the moral responsibility to think through for yourself the basis of your ethical views.

Feelings are often given as a basis for moral decision-making. Many claim that if it feels good or right, it is moral; if it feels bad or wrong, it is immoral. A "gut check" is probably a good idea when you are faced with an ethical dilemma, but it is doubtful that mere feelings are enough to provide a solid basis for making ethical choices. Feelings are notoriously fickle; they change all the time. Can it really be true that the morality of something changes with your mood swings? Your choice is a moral choice at one point, when you are feeling euphoric and happy about it. Is it possible that it could suddenly become immoral a few minutes later when you feel shamed and remorseful?

Our feelings are an important part of making ethical or moral decisions, but they are inadequate as the sole basis for such decisions. It does not take long to see that this is true. If a person has no conscience and therefore feels perfectly fine about defrauding or abusing other human beings, does their lack of the feelings of shame or remorse make the abusive or fraudulent behavior acceptable? Very few would answer, "Yes."

Some of the world's greatest minds have thought deeply on the moral basis for our actions. Over time, the most influential perspectives have been debated and refined into a few ethical "schools of thought." In this book, we will consider the major theories that have lasted through the ages. Each theory is worth serious consideration, because each connects in some very fundamental way with our ethical understanding of the world. The four theories we will consider are:

- Utilitarianism

- Kantian ethics

- Justice ethics

- Virtue ethics

These theories have considerable agreement concerning what is morally right or wrong, but there are also areas of disagreement. While the overlap among the theories is interesting and encouraging, it is also important to note the ways in which these theories differ from one another. The next four chapters will explain each theory, noting apparent strengths and potential weaknesses. The rest of the chapters model the kind of analyses you can take to a variety of ethical situations specific to hospitality and tourism. At the end of these chapters, short case studies are provided for your own analysis. A deep, thoughtful consideration of ethical issues can make us all more aware and better able to make wise decisions in the world of work.

Chapter Questions

1. What is the loyal agent's argument? Give an example of a loyal agent.

2. Explain the difference between individual self-interest and collective self-interest.

3. What is the "prisoner's dilemma?"

4. Is it true that high ethical and social responsibility standards always lead to higher profits? Explain your answer.

5. When might you not be held responsible for unethical behavior?

6. What are mitigating circumstances? Give an example of a mitigating circumstance.

7. People often rely on their "gut reaction" when making a moral decision. Will a gut reaction help you make a moral decision? Why or why not?

Thinking Exercise

Have you ever been in a "loyal agent's" dilemma? What were the circumstances? What did you do? Would you make the same choice today that you did then? Explain your answer.

2

Utilitarianism:
The Greatest Good

SOME ETHICAL THEORIES argue that the *consequences* of an action make it either moral or immoral. Thus, an action that leads to beneficial consequences is right or moral, and one that leads to harmful consequences is wrong or immoral. All theories of this nature are known as consequentialist theories, because of their dependence on consequences as criteria for moral rightness or wrongness.

The most influential consequentialist theory is known as utilitarianism. Utilitarianism takes its name from the concept of "utility," meaning the benefits to be derived from an action or situation. In its most simplified form, utilitarianism holds that an action is morally justified to the extent that it maximizes benefits and minimizes harm or costs. Thus, the one moral thing to do in any situation is that action that can be reasonably seen to provide the greatest *net* benefit for all concerned, when the expected costs are subtracted from the expected benefits. To do something else is to behave unethically, and the more an alternative action maximizes net costs or net harm, the more immoral it becomes. The shorthand often used to describe utilitarianism is that it calls for "the greatest good for the greatest number of people."

It is important to note that utilitarianism does not say that the moral action is the one that maximizes the benefits or happiness *of the person doing the action*. It must be the benefits and happiness of *all*—each person counts equally. Thus, any attempt to use utilitarianism to justify selfish behavior at the expense of the greatest good for the whole society would be a misuse of the doctrine. Another common misconception is the belief that utilitarianism takes into account only the *immediate* consequences of an action. This is wrong—utilitarianism clearly states that *all* consequences must be counted, and this includes both short-term and long-term consequences, to the extent that these can be foreseen.

This certainly seems to make a lot of sense because we generally approve of promoting the general welfare. But there are a number of questions that must be answered before we can be certain that this is a valid and workable ethical theory.

What Is the "Good?"

What is the "good" we are trying to maximize? If different people have different ideas of the "good," we will not get anywhere until we clear that up. Some argue that wealth is the "good." But others believe that wealth can be corrupting and is unworthy of being the ultimate aim in life. Some equate power with the "good."

But again, many scorn power and believe that "the good life" has next to nothing to do with having power over others. Similar disagreements occur over other possible candidates for what makes the good life: fame, a good reputation, etc.

Utilitarians usually state that the greatest good means the greatest happiness. They back up this claim by pointing out that everybody wants to be happy—it is the one universal thing that everybody desires and agrees is a good thing.

So if everybody desires happiness, perhaps happiness is the universal good that provides a satisfactory criterion for determining what is ethical or moral and what is unethical or immoral. The moral thing to do is whatever maximizes happiness and minimizes unhappiness; the immoral thing to do is whatever minimizes happiness and maximizes unhappiness.

Jeremy Bentham: Pleasures and Pains

Jeremy Bentham (1748–1832), an English philosopher, is widely credited with founding utilitarianism.[1] Bentham argues that happiness and unhappiness are identical to the amount of *pleasure* or *pain* experienced. A life of pleasure is a happy life; a life of pain is an unhappy one. Bentham determines the morality of an action by measuring the quantity of pleasure and the quantity of pain it will produce. After the two quantities are determined and the smaller is subtracted from the larger, you can then measure it morally against other possible actions. The right (or moral, or ethical) action is the one that provides the highest *net* quantity of pleasure. The more net unhappiness an action produces, the more immoral it is.

A number of major objections have been made to Bentham's argument. First, it is difficult (if not impossible) to quantify or measure "units" of pleasure and pain. Thus, the system is unworkable. Second, it is argued that pleasure and pain are the wrong measures of happiness and unhappiness. For example, could it really be true that you would have a happy or a good life if you felt nothing but pleasure in an unthinking haze as you were hooked to a machine pumping heroin into your addicted body continuously over the course of a long life? What if you lived permanently in an elegant spa resort with no cares or worries, but also no purpose or goals—just a seemingly aimless existence? Would either of these really be preferable to the life of a thinking, intelligent person who experienced more pain along with the less intense pleasures of a more normal life? Put another way, would you prefer the life of a satisfied pig experiencing pleasure after pleasure to the life of an intelligent human experiencing a greater degree of dissatisfaction and pain, but who accomplishes great things?

Defenders of Bentham answer these objections by noting that it may be difficult to quantify pains and pleasures, or to put a value on them, but it can be done—at least in an approximate way. In fact, it is done all the time in what economists and businesspeople call "cost-benefit" analyses. Hotels and airlines frequently do cost-benefit analyses to aid in decisions on whether or not to follow a particular course of action. Restaurants that offer "free entrée with purchase of another en-

---

[1] See Jeremy Bentham, *The Principles of Morals and Legislation* (Amherst, N.Y.: Prometheus Books, 1988). This book was originally published in 1789.

trée" probably do so on the basis of a cost-benefit analysis. The cost of the second entrée may be quite small compared to the benefit to be gained from all the additional business (more customers, more spending on appetizers, desserts, drinks, etc.) that results from the special offer.

Insurance companies use a cost-benefit analysis when they try to put a value on "intangible" things (such as loss of companionship, or loss of a family heirloom) to compensate those insured under their policies. Insurance companies also put a value on the loss of a limb, or even the loss of life. While this may be upsetting or repulsive to some people, defenders of the practice argue that it is inescapable if restitution is to be made for loss of a loved one or loss of particular body parts. So, in general, a defender of Bentham would probably say that quantifying all the pleasures and pains in life may be difficult, but it is not impossible in principle. We must simply do the best we can.

This may or may not be a satisfactory answer to the first objection, but the second objection, that "happiness" over the long run means much more than simply pleasure and the absence of pain, is more difficult to answer. Consider the *qualitative* difference between the life of a mentally handicapped adult who laughs continuously at simple pleasures but has no ability to think coherently about the world, and the pleasures of a thinking adult in control of his or her life. Wouldn't we find the life of the latter to be a "happier" life, in the long-term sense of being a "good life" or a "fulfilled life" than that of the former? Would a vegetative state of numerous pleasures and few pains (but little or no thinking), really be preferable to a thoughtful life full of both pleasures and pains?

John Stuart Mill: The Quality of Happiness

This objection to Bentham is a serious problem because most of us find some pleasures and pains to be *qualitatively* superior to others. Nineteenth century utilitarian philosopher John Stuart Mill attempted to answer this objection by incorporating into utilitarianism qualitative differences between pleasures. Mill states:

> It is better to be a human being dissatisfied than a pig satisfied; better to be Socrates (*famous ancient Greek philosopher – editor's note*) dissatisfied than a fool satisfied. And if the fool, or the pig, are of different opinion, it is because they only know their own side of the question. The other party to the comparison knows both sides.[2]

This reply has not satisfied some critics of utilitarianism, who believe that the introduction of "qualitative" pleasures and pains undermines the whole attempt to reduce the good and bad things in life into interchangeable, tradable units. First, they would argue that we cannot really make a meaningful comparison between, say, the pleasure one person gets from watching a pornographic film with the pleasure another person gets from attending an Italian opera or reading a book of philosophy. Put another way, we cannot make a meaningful comparison

---

[2] John Stuart Mill, *Utilitarianism* (1863). Quote taken from selection reprinted in Shari Collins-Chobanian, ed., *Ethical Challenges to Business as Usual* (Upper Saddle River, N.J.: Pearson Prentice Hall, 2005), p. 21.

between the pleasure one person gets from a gourmet steak dinner with the pleasure another person gets from a hamburger, milkshake, and french fries. There is no common unit of measurement that can quantify qualitatively different experiences of pleasure.

Second, they would argue that some things, such as freedom, human rights, justice, and life itself are more precious than any pleasures we could turn into quantifiable units. We should not be willing to trade these things away for a certain quantity of pleasure, and any ethical theory that tells us to do so is deficient, say these critics.

Most modern utilitarians believe that Bentham's equation of happiness with simple pleasure and the absence of pain is too narrow. Therefore they either agree with John Stuart Mill by making qualitative distinctions between types of pleasures and pains, or they view happiness as something more complex than a simple pleasure-pain calculus. But they do insist that the maximization of human happiness (or human benefits) and the minimization of human unhappiness (or human harm, or costs) is the goal of morality. This is the essence of utilitarianism.

Strong Points of Utilitarianism

Despite the objections raised so far, utilitarianism seems to have a lot going for it as an ethical theory. It makes sense that we have a moral duty to behave in ways that create as many benefits for human society as possible, and to avoid as much as possible the harms or costs to the entire society. We frequently justify actions on this basis. So there is no doubt that utilitarianism has a strong hold on our moral thinking and reasoning. Decisions are made every day on the basis of utilitarian calculations, especially when there are trade-offs involved in doing one thing or another. Should we spend scarce health care resources on buying an extremely expensive kidney dialysis machine, or should those dollars be spent on flu vaccinations for a few thousand children in the public school system? In a hotel, should we fix the refrigeration unit that seems to be acting up, or should we refurbish the lobby? By calculating the net benefit of taking one course of action over another, and then choosing the action that provides the greatest net benefit, we are clearly using a utilitarian decision-making method.

A Major Criticism of Utilitarianism

There is another extremely serious objection to utilitarianism that many believe makes it unacceptable as a complete basis for our moral thinking. This objection is that utilitarianism would justify actions that violate other people's rights and/or lead to injustices.

For example, consider a situation where a large family decides to enslave an adopted twelve-year-old child and force her to do virtually all of the labor in the family home. She is not allowed to step outside the family house, and is periodically beaten for not working hard enough. She toils intensively for about sixteen hours a day, seven days a week. She will not live long because of the overwork, and her existence is miserable. However, ten family members live in ease and great comfort because of her hard work. They get immense pleasure and happiness from the situation because they are freed from all work. They read books, develop their talents, play games, enjoy a comfortable life of interesting and fun pursuits. In short, they live "the good life." But it is all done on the basis of enslaving the adopted daughter.

The enjoyment of the ten family members, if it can be put into measurable "units," may far outweigh the misery of the one enslaved girl when the units of happiness and unhappiness are counted up. In this case, utilitarianism would seem to condone such a family situation. Yet, it is clearly a violation of a person's rights and a great injustice. A person who is enslaved loses the right to control his or her destiny. He or she has lost the most basic human right—the right to be free. It also offends our sense of justice; slavery does not treat people in a just or fair manner. The slave is discriminated against and denied freedom for no morally justified reason. Slavery is inherently *exploitative*. It can never be morally justified because it denies basic human rights and is inherently unjust.

Thus, a very fundamental objection to utilitarianism is that it counts only the benefits and burdens produced by actions or by social arrangements, *but fails to take into account the distribution* of benefits and burdens. It therefore condones unjust situations where benefits and burdens are distributed unfairly. It also fails to take into account individual entitlements to basic freedom of choice and to well being, thereby approving violations of basic human rights.

This is a very serious objection, but utilitarians do not find it to be persuasive. One reply is that examples such as the one just given are fanciful and not accurate to any real life situation. A defender of utilitarianism could argue that the benefit to other family members is so small and inconsequential (a little more free time) that, even with their great numbers, the total additional happiness or benefit to them in no way counterbalances the horrible consequences to the enslaved child.

Furthermore, the *long-term* consequences, including indirect consequences, of such an arrangement would be extremely detrimental. Family members who can adapt to a situation of domestic enslavement of one of their own will become insensitive to cruel treatment in general, and will engage in such behavior elsewhere, further increasing the misery in the world and decreasing the sum total of human happiness. In fact, they would argue, the case is obvious: the enslavement does *not* bring about the greatest happiness for the greatest number. Therefore, it is immoral and would never be condoned by a full utilitarian investigation and moral judgment.

This answer may be satisfactory, but it is not clear to many that it will *always* turn out to be the case that violations of an individual's human rights lead to a net decrease in human happiness, or overall human benefit. Might there not be cases where the greatest happiness does come from unjust treatment, or from violating the rights of individuals?

Two Types of Utilitarianism

Some utilitarians have modified their system in an attempt to take more account of individual human rights and of our notion of justice or fairness. The modification distinguishes between the traditional form of utilitarianism that we have been considering, called *act utilitarianism*, and a second type called *rule utilitarianism*. Recall that the traditional form of utilitarianism (act utilitarianism) applies the "greatest good" principle to *individual acts*. Rule utilitarianism applies this principle not to individual acts, but to *moral rules of conduct*.

According to rule utilitarianism, we need to look at which moral rules lead to the greatest happiness for the greatest number. What would the consequences be if everyone were to follow a certain moral rule? If universal acceptance and adherence to the rule would lead to the greatest happiness for the greatest number, it is a justified moral rule and we all should follow it. If we do that, it is argued, we will never justify injustices or violations of human rights.

To see why that is so, consider the child slavery example we have just noted. Which of the following general rules would lead to the greatest happiness for the greatest number: (1) People are allowed to enslave other human beings; or (2) People are forbidden to enslave other human beings? Rule utilitarians would argue that the answer is obvious. As a general rule, Rule #2 will obviously lead to the greater good (more happiness) than Rule #1. Therefore, we must all follow Rule #2.

Rule utilitarians thus answer the objection that utilitarianism fails to account for individual rights or for our notions of justice by limiting the utilitarian calculus of happiness and unhappiness to *the moral rules by which we live, not to individual actions*. And, they argue, we will see that the best rules (that is, the ones that lead to the greatest happiness) are invariably those that respect individual human rights and build in fair and equal treatment of everyone. Individual exceptions, such as a family wishing to enslave or mistreat an adopted daughter, are not allowed because the *universal* adoption of enslavement would definitely lead to less happiness and more unhappiness.

Critics are not necessarily satisfied with this argument. They have two objections. First, they argue that it is not necessarily clear in all instances that rules requiring respect for individual rights or fair and equal treatment of all *do* lead to the greatest quantity of happiness. And if they do not, a utilitarian would condone violations of individual rights or injustices. The critics argue that respect for human rights and just treatment of others is right regardless of the impact on happiness or unhappiness. In other words, they challenge the claim that maximum happiness is the *ultimate* moral goal: human rights and fair treatment are *independent* moral goals that are more important than even happiness.

Second, some critics argue that rule utilitarianism is really no different from act utilitarianism. To understand this objection, ask the following question: do the moral rules in a rule utilitarian system allow for exceptions in some circumstances? If they do (for example, if we adopt the rule, "People are forbidden to enslave other human beings, *except in those cases where the sum total of human happiness is increased by the enslavement*,") we are right back to act utilitarianism. People will still have to sum up the happiness and unhappiness resulting from each act of enslavement, and decide the morality of it on that basis. This is no different than act utilitarianism.

Not allowing exceptions to the rule would undermine the very basis of utilitarianism. For example, not allowing any exceptions to the "no slavery" rule might lead to a situation where "the greatest happiness for the greatest number of people" is not achieved, since exceptional cases may occur where enslavement does lead to the greatest quantity of happiness.

Thus, some critics contend that rule utilitarianism is either act utilitarianism in disguise (a "wolf in sheep's clothing"), or it is an abandonment of utilitarianism altogether. The rule utilitarian who does not allow exceptions to general moral rules will argue, of course, that utilitarianism has not been abandoned, merely modified and applied at the level of *rule-making* rather than the level of *acting*.

Utilitarianism: A Summary

As you can see, there are many controversies surrounding utilitarianism as an ethical system. However, utilitarianism is a very powerful ethical system that fits quite well with many of the ways we make moral decisions. Very few would want to argue that unhappiness is better than happiness, for example. And most would agree that every person's happiness counts equally, so our attempts to promote happiness must take everybody impartially into account, not simply our own individual happiness.

However, there are two major objections to utilitarianism, as we have noted. One is that it attempts to turn everything into a measurable value, and therefore does not deal well with values that are difficult to measure. Are some types of pleasure or happiness *qualitatively* better than others? If so, can this really be accounted for in the utilitarian system? Second, it does not seem to deal well with situations where individual rights or justice matter, although some utilitarians have tried to fix this problem by applying the "greatest happiness" or the "greatest good" evaluation only to rules, not to individual actions.

Now that you are familiar with the arguments for and against utilitarianism, you should think these arguments through and decide if it is a satisfactory ethical system to guide your conduct. Before you can completely make up your mind, however, you should become familiar with other ethical theories.

Chapter Questions

1. When does utilitarianism consider an action to be morally justified?

2. What is the "shorthand" statement that is often used to characterize utilitarianism?

3. Who is the philosopher credited with founding utilitarianism? What was the argument that he used to determine the morality of one's actions?

4. What was the argument John Stuart Mill used to answer the critics of Bentham's version of utilitarianism?

5. A hotel manger wants to refurbish the dining room but also knows that the ceiling tiles in the hallway must be replaced because of a recently broken pipe (that is now fixed). What factors would make you choose one course of action over the other? Why?

6. Do you agree or disagree with the criticisms of utilitarianism? Explain your answer.

7. What arguments would a utilitarian use against slavery? How would a utilitarian argue for slavery?

8. What is the difference between an act utilitarian and a rule utilitarian? Which is superior to the other? Why?

Thinking exercise

Apply a utilitarian analysis to ethical issues that arose in a work situation you have experienced. Describe the circumstances. What was the specific problem and how did you handle it? Did your solution coincide with a utilitarian solution? Explain your answer.

3

Kantian Ethics: Duties and Rights

IMMANUEL KANT, an 18th Century German philosopher (1724–1804), developed an approach to ethics very different from utilitarianism in his famous book, *Foundations of the Metaphysics of Morals* (1785).[1] Kant argued that the consequences of an action are irrelevant to a moral evaluation of that action. Therefore, Kant is not a consequentialist, since he believes consequences to be morally irrelevant. Instead, Kant's ethical theory is a prime example of what we call a *deontological* ethical theory. "Deontological" is taken from the Greek word "deon," which means duty. Deontological ethical theories argue that actions are moral or immoral because of their very nature, not because of their consequences. For Kant, their nature stems from the type of rules they follow, and it is on the basis of the rule followed that we can morally judge an action.

It's the Motive that Counts

To understand this important difference between Kant and a utilitarian, consider the following situation. Two wealthy hotel owners give money to charity. One of them does it because he considers it his duty to do so, having been more fortunate in life than some others who are in desperate need. The other does it only because his name and picture will appear in the media, enhancing his status in the community. This owner seeks maximum exposure and makes sure that his giving is widely publicized. The first owner makes no effort to bring attention to his charitable giving, because he does not consider that relevant to his reasons for giving in the first place.

How would we morally judge the actions of these two individuals? Assuming that their wealth was similar and that their charitable giving was of the same magnitude, if they both gave to the same or similar charities and those charities did an equivalent amount of good for the poor and the suffering with those donations, a utilitarian would say that their actions are morally equal. Since they have identical

---

[1] See Immanuel Kant, *Groundwork of the Metaphysics of Morals* (New York: Cambridge University Press, 1998). This book was originally published in 1785. (Note also that different translations of this book from the German original use different words for the first word in the title. In this book we follow some translators in calling it *"Foundations"* of the Metaphysics of Morals, while the translated version in this footnote calls it *"Groundwork"* of the Metaphysics of Morals.)

consequences, they are of exactly the same moral worth. Kant, on the other hand, would say that their actions do not have equal moral worth. He would argue that the consequences of their actions (the good done by the charities with the money they contribute) are morally irrelevant. Instead, Kant would judge the actions of the first owner as moral, because they were done for the right reasons. The actions of the second owner have no moral worth even though they result in good for the world, because they were done for the wrong reasons. The actions of the first owner are by their very nature morally praiseworthy, while those of the second are not, because the self-serving motivation behind them changes their nature into simply another effort at self-promotion (which is not a morally praiseworthy action).

For Kant, it is the motivation behind an action that makes it morally worth praising or condemning. Moral actions are undertaken out of a sense of *duty*—which means you do it because you know that it is "the right thing to do."

Actions that are undertaken simply because you enjoy them, for example, do not take on a moral character, even if they result in many positive benefits for others. We may be happy and appreciative when we receive excellent service in a restaurant. Our appreciation is not a moral appreciation. It is more like our appreciation for warm weather, or abundant resources, or other things that make our lives more comfortable but which we do not judge morally—positively or negatively.

What Is Our Duty?

If Kant is right that it is the motivation that counts, and if the motivation must be a desire to do what we feel to be our moral duty, how do we determine what is our duty? Kant argues that this can be derived from our unique nature as human beings. As human beings we are uniquely *rational* in a way that all other living creatures on earth are not. We alone can reason, and our ability to reason requires us to be logical and consistent. To be logical and consistent, we have to be able and willing to make the basic rules by which we operate into *universal* rules that everyone could and should follow. If we cannot do that, we are illogical and inconsistent. Furthermore, Kant would argue, we are immoral, because we are not granting to other human beings the same freedom and the same status as a rational human being that we are claiming for ourselves. This general claim is the basis of Kant's ethical system. He formulated this claim in a couple of different ways, and it will be much clearer if we consider two of those formulations.

Categorical Imperative: First Formulation

Kant called his formulations of the basic rule of morality the *categorical imperative*. By an "imperative" he means a command that you must follow if you wish to be moral. By "categorical" he means that the command must be followed no matter what, not merely if it is convenient or if it has a certain set of consequences. There are no "ifs" to a categorical rule or imperative; it must be followed under all circumstances. The categorical imperative is *the* rule, or command, that we all must follow at all times in all places under all circumstances—if we wish to act morally.

According to Kant: "Act only on that maxim whereby thou canst at the same time will that it should become a universal law."[2] This means that you must act in such a way that you would want the rule you are following to be a universal one that everyone should follow. For example, if you want to cheat a guest and pocket the money, you have to be able to "will it" (or want it) that everyone cheats. If you want to break a promise (for example, a promise that room numbers will not to be given out for any reason), you must will it that everyone breaks promises. If you want to commit robbery, murder, rape, or a number of other actions we think to be immoral, you must be able to will it to be the case that they are universally done.

Kant would argue that you cannot will it to be the case that such actions be universally undertaken. This is true, not necessarily because you would not like the consequences (although that certainly would be true), but because it would be self-contradictory and impossible to actually make these into universal practices. Universal breaking of promises would undermine the very meaning of making a promise, and thus it would destroy the entire practice of promise-making, and thus it is self-contradictory. The same is true for cheating, for deceptive practices, and for robbery, whose universal practice undermines the very meaning of owning property, etc.

Therefore, Kant contends that the categorical imperative supplies the universal rule, or command, that we all must follow to be moral. Those who are familiar with the golden rule (*"Do unto others as you would have them do unto you"*) have probably noticed the very close similarity between it and Kant's categorical imperative. However similar, they are not identical. The golden rule depends on which consequences you want, while Kant claims his categorical imperative does not (although this is a point of some controversy among philosophers). It may not be identical, but the categorical imperative is so close to the golden rule that there would be little, if any, difference in practice.

Categorical Imperative: Second Formulation

Kant has a second formulation of his categorical imperative that highlights another aspect of it. Recall that he derives the categorical imperative from the fact that human beings are unique among animals—we alone have reason and therefore we alone are able (and required) to act rationally. Only a rational creature capable of using reason to decide what to do (and what not to do) is capable of being truly free. Animals who live according to instincts are not free in the same way that we are, because they cannot use reason to freely choose their actions; they must blindly follow their instincts. But human beings, as rational creatures, are by their very nature free because their rationality allows them to contemplate alternative actions and to freely choose the one they will undertake.

Because of the unique status of human beings (i.e., of rational creatures), Kant asserts that they, and they alone, have *unconditional* worth. Every human being,

---

2 Immanuel Kant, *Foundations of the Metaphysics of Morals* (1785). Quote taken from selection reprinted in Shari Collins-Chobarian, ed., *Ethical Challenges to Business as Usual* (Upper Saddle River, N.J.: Pearson Prentice Hall, 2005), p. 32.

and every human life, is unconditionally valuable in a way that mere objects or tools, or plants and other animals are not. We feel free to use tools and objects with little regard to the impact on them. If I damage a tool when I do a job, I can simply throw the tool away and get another one. The tool itself has no moral claims on me, and I have not committed an immoral act if I use the tool merely as a means to accomplish some other end.

Kant asserts that it would be immoral to treat another human being that way. If I fail to see each human being as an end-in-himself or end-in-herself, I am denying that human being the freedom that he or she has by virtue of being a rational (and therefore free) being. I have degraded that person from the status of a human being to the status of a "thing," and I have "used" them in a manner that is both immoral and contrary to the categorical imperative, since we could not will it to be the case that all human beings degrade and use each other in this manner. Therefore, Kant comes up with a second formulation of the categorical imperative: "So act as to treat humanity, whether in thine own person or in that of any other, in every case as an end withal, never as means only."[3] This means that you must never use a person just for your own purposes. Instead, you must treat every human being as someone of independent moral worth, with an equal claim to freely decide his or her own life choices. To deny this freedom to all is to violate a fundamental duty we have to one another. It would be immoral, and it would be a violation of the first formulation of the categorical imperative since it would be impossible to will it to be the case that everyone universally "used" each other this way. Practical life would be impossible, and it would be a self-contradictory negation to further human (free, independent) life by denying a human being a free, independent life.

Strengths of Kant's System

At this point, we hope you see what a powerful, useful ethical system Kant's theory can be. It definitely coincides with some of our most deeply held moral beliefs: the sanctity of human life, the need to be impartial and to not make exceptions for oneself, and the duty we owe to others to treat each person as a "person," and not as a "thing." It also explains our tendency to morally judge the actions of others on the basis of their intentions or motives, not merely on the basis of the consequences of their actions, as utilitarianism does.

Kant and the Concept of "Rights"

Kant speaks frequently of the "duty" we owe to each other. The word "duty" has a counterpart on the other side: if I have a duty toward you, you have a "right" to demand from me that I fulfill that duty. Thus, the concept of "rights" follows easily from Kant's ethical system. As we have seen previously, utilitarianism seems to have a problem accounting for, or dealing adequately with, our notion of "rights."

---

[3] Immanuel Kant, *Foundations of the Metaphysics of Morals* (1785). Quote taken from selection reprinted in Shari Collins-Chobarian, ed., *Ethical Challenges to Business as Usual* (Upper Saddle River, N.J.: Pearson Prentice Hall, 2005), p. 33.

But an ethical theory built on the concept of duty, as is Kant's theory, has no such problem.

What exactly is a "right?" When we say that someone's rights were violated, what do we mean? To have a right to something means to be *entitled* to it. Rights are individual entitlements.

We are primarily concerned with moral rights in this chapter, but the same meaning of an individual entitlement holds when we refer to legal rights. Legal rights are claims that an individual can make against others, based on the legal system. If I have a legal right to sell my hotel or to order you off my hotel property, these rights are granted by the government's property laws, and I can use the legal system to enforce those legal rights. When we refer to moral rights or human rights, we are referring to entitlements that are grounded in a moral code or system. Kant would say, for instance, that we all have a moral right to not be treated as mere "things"—we have a right to be treated as free, rational, independent, thinking beings.

Negative Rights and Positive Rights

A right is something that you are entitled to have others observe. Negative rights arise when others may be prohibited or forbidden from interfering with your ability to freely choose a certain course of action. An example would be the right to privacy. If such a moral right exists under certain circumstances, it requires that others observe a moral duty to leave a person alone in those circumstances, if the person wishes to be left alone. Another example would be the disposition of one's property. If I have an absolute property right over something, I have a right to buy it, sell it, change it, destroy it, or do as I please with it, free from external interference. Negative rights require that we leave people alone to freely choose a course of action, as long as they respect the rights of others to equally choose freely.

The rights that require others to do or provide something are known as positive rights. Examples would be the moral (and possibly legal) right to work, the right to have enough food and shelter to survive, the right to adequate health care, the right to an education at public expense, and the like. Full-time hotel employees can expect to receive compensation and benefits that allow them to live at a decent level. These are examples of positive rights.

A person who has a positive right to something is entitled to expect others to undertake some action or to provide something, not merely to refrain from interfering with something being attempted. There is often controversy about positive rights—some say that there are no such rights at all or that they are very few in number. We will not enter into this controversy here, other than to note that in advanced industrial countries, at least some positive rights are generally conceded. For example, the right of all children to a free public education for a certain number of years, or the right of all citizens to get some type of health care, etc.

Kant's ethical system clearly imposes a duty to respect a number of negative rights. The categorical imperative requires that we treat each human being as free and equal in the pursuit of their interests. Therefore, assault, rape, murder, robbery, lying, fraud, extortion, cheating, and the like are all prohibited as interferences with the right to be treated as a human being (a rational creature) and not a thing.

Also, freedom of speech, the right to privacy, freedom of association, and freedom of thought must not be interfered with for the same reason.

Kant's ethical system can also be plausibly interpreted to require respect for certain positive rights. As one philosopher writing on business ethics puts it:

> ... human beings have a clear interest in being helped by being provided with the work, food, clothing, housing, and medical care they need to live on when they cannot provide these for themselves. Suppose we agree that we would not be willing to have everyone (especially ourselves) deprived of such help when it is needed, and that such help is necessary if a person's capacity to choose freely is to develop and even survive. If so, then no individual should be deprived of such help. That is, human beings have *positive* rights to the work, food, clothing, housing, and medical care they need to live on when they cannot provide these for themselves and when these are available.[4]

Despite the strengths of Kant's system, it is not without its critics. One of the main criticisms is that it is very hard to apply to actual situations. It does not give us much practical guidance in the most difficult matters. A second criticism is that it may lead to conflicting duties, whereby observing one Kantian duty would require violating another Kantian duty. A third criticism, made by utilitarians, is that Kant's system is simply wrong in ignoring the consequences of actions when making moral judgments.

Applicability

Some critics claim that Kant's system does not really give us much guidance in most difficult situations. For example, suppose a restaurant manager is trying to decide the ethical policy to follow regarding provision of wages, tips, and benefits for each of the restaurant's front and back-of-the-house employees. From Kant, we know that every employee must be given the moral status of an "end-in-himself" or an "end-in-herself," which means that each employee cannot be degraded to the status of a "thing." Each deserves equal and independent moral status, with unconditional worth. Clearly, that would rule out forced labor or paying people less than it requires to survive, but those are the obvious cases. How much provision of benefits is required? What wage is required? Inevitably there will be all kinds of trade-offs in making decisions of this nature, and critics claim that Kant is really not very helpful in making this type of decision.

A defender of Kant would reply that the application of any ethical system is never easy. We saw the same thing with utilitarianism in the objection that quantifying happiness (or benefits) is difficult, if not impossible. Despite the difficulty in making precise judgments for every situation, a Kantian could argue that the basic principles required by Kant's system are clear enough. For example, denying employees, especially the lowest paid employees like bussers and new servers, sufficient resources to live a life of freedom and autonomy is immoral. Exactly

---

[4] Manuel G. Velasquez, *Business Ethics: Concepts and Cases* (Upper Saddle River, N.J.: Prentice Hall, 2002), p. 101.

where to draw the line in terms of pay and benefit levels may be subject to debate, but the basic principle is clear enough.

Conflicting Duties

Kantian duties may conflict with each other. Kant's emphasis on rigid, unwavering duties irrespective of consequences seems to run into difficulties in situations where fulfilling one obligation requires not fulfilling another obligation. An example of this difficulty is the permissibility of being deceitful in certain circumstances. Suppose you know a couple and the husband beats his wife frequently, sometimes severely. One evening, she calls you in a panic and asks if she can stay overnight at your house. She says that her husband is on the rampage and is coming home shortly with the intention of beating her so badly that she fears for her life. You agree to put her up for the night. Later that evening, her husband shows up at your door in an apparent rage, asking if his wife is there. You are fairly certain that if you honestly reply that she is there, the husband will forcibly enter your house (which he will be able to do because he has superior force over whatever weapons or capabilities you have) and drag his wife away for at least a severe beating and possibly permanent injury or death.

Imagine a similar scenario, but placed into a hospitality context. You and Joyce both work at the Bedrock Hotel. Herman, the general manager, continuously sexually harasses Joyce. It gets so bad that Joyce begins to fear for her own safety. She starts looking for another job, but she makes you promise that you won't tell Herman. You promise. The next day Herman asks you exactly that, "Is Joyce looking for another job?"

Recall that Kant derives from the categorical imperative a clear rule against lying under any circumstances. Since you cannot make lying into a universal principle, you must always speak honestly. On the other hand, you have a duty to each individual to protect his or her humanity. That means you have a duty to the wife, or to your friend, or to a fellow employee, etc., to protect his or her freedom and autonomy. Certainly it means protecting her from imminent attack and possibly death. In either case, which course of action should be followed? Should you lie and tell the husband that his wife is not there? Should you lie and tell the boss that Joyce is not looking for another job? In both cases that would break one Kantian duty. Or, should you tell the truth? That means breaking another Kantian duty.

The point of this exercise is to show that we can get into situations where fulfilling one duty requires breaking another. In real life circumstances, there are many such situations, and you can probably come up with a number of other examples. The argument against Kant is that his system provides no guidance when duties conflict with each other. His rigid, unwavering rules (such as a prohibition on lying) provide little leeway in situations with conflicting duties.

One possible reply by a Kantian is that the rule against lying would have to be reformulated in a circumstance such as the one stated above. Could we make it a universal rule that everyone could lie under those circumstances? Perhaps we could if we could determine that the duty to protect the life and well being of others is more fundamental than the duty to not lie. Such an argument could be made by a Kantian, because the duty to protect life and health is more closely related than is the duty not to lie to the fundamental core principle of the second statement of the categorical imperative: the duty not to deny the humanity (freedom and autonomy) of other human beings. Clearly, you are denying a person's humanity more if you allow them to be beaten and possibly killed than you are if you lie to someone.

This may be a satisfactory answer, but it certainly destroys the initial simplicity of Kant's system. One of the attractions of Kant's system is that it does not allow rationalizations and exceptions to basic moral rules all the time, unlike utilitarianism (at least act utilitarianism), which some claim allows too much leeway to rationalize away immoral behavior. If Kant were to allow numerous exceptions to the basic duties and rules derived from his system ("Don't lie." "Don't cheat." etc.), his system would slip back in the direction of less moral certainty and frequent moral ambiguity. Yet, this may be required if he is to satisfactorily deal with situations where duties appear to conflict with each other.

Are Consequences Irrelevant?

A final objection to Kant's model is that it is just plain wrong when it ignores the consequences of actions while making a moral judgment. Utilitarians, of course, make this criticism. They argue that Kant's emphasis on the rights of individuals goes too far, because it may lead to situations where the welfare of the society as a whole is being sacrificed. A Kantian, of course, would argue that the rights of the individual must be protected against the will of the majority, and that those rights are more precious than any amount of public welfare. This is an issue that appears to be a philosophical difference of opinion.

Libertarianism

Before we leave Kant, we should perhaps note some philosophers who operate from a "rights" perspective that is different from that of Kant. These philosophers, known as *libertarian philosophers*, believe that Kant is on the right track when he uses duties and rights as the basis of his system. However, they have a particular notion of rights that sets them apart. Libertarians accept Kant's claim that all human beings have a right to freedom and autonomy, and, therefore, they endorse negative rights, that is, rights against coercion.

However, libertarians deny that there are any positive rights. We have no obligation to provide anything to anybody else, in this view. Libertarians treat an individual's property as an extension of the person, so one's property is not to be interfered with, and attempts to do so constitute unethical coercion. Therefore, individuals of this persuasion oppose taxes as immoral coercion, since it is an involuntary taking away of one's property. They likewise tend to oppose governmental social welfare programs. They condemn governmental requirements that those with more money or possessions contribute the resources needed to provide for those with less. Any such requirement is seen as an immoral violation of the rights (property rights) of the wealthier person who is being taxed to support those with little or no income.

On a broader scale, this view argues that the only morally permissible transfer of money or possessions between people is voluntary exchanges, or voluntary giving. People can make a "contract" with each other, and agree to buy or sell property, but anything beyond contractual rights that involves the taking of money or property involuntarily would be seen as a violation of the owner's individual rights.

Libertarianism has a certain popular following. Milton Friedman, a well-known economist, expresses a mild version of it. Friedman argues that business executives have no obligation beyond the obligation to make the most money possible for the company's owners, as long as they abide by the society's basic laws and moral standards. "Freedom" is an attractive goal, and the libertarian claim to uphold freedom has an attraction for many.

Objections to Libertarianism

However, there are two major problems with libertarianism. The first is that it seems to ignore the fact that freedom for one person will mean constraints on others. Freedom for one inevitably means the loss of some kind of freedom for others. Thus, any particular freedom must be justified, since it implies restrictions on the freedom of others. For example, the freedom of a corporation (based on its property rights) to utilize its property to pollute the atmosphere is a restriction on the freedom (or right) of citizens to breathe unpolluted air, or to have healthy living conditions. Another example would be a hotel with a disco that brings loud revelers through a residential area until very late hours. Which freedom takes precedence?

Libertarians have a difficult time answering this question. The answer that most people would approve (that our freedom to breathe unpolluted air takes precedence or that we have the right to a quiet environment after certain hours) may begin to unravel the entire libertarian argument. The more involuntary restrictions (particularly restrictions on property rights) that are allowed, the further we move from the state of affairs most cherished by libertarians—few or no restrictions on property rights.

The second problem with libertarianism is the extremely restricted view of freedom that it seems to have. In general, apart from freedom against aggression or bodily assault, the main freedom of concern to libertarians is the freedom to own and control one's property. But this is a very narrow view of freedom. For example, is a destitute individual who is starving to death really free, simply because he or she has the "right" to own property? This seems to be a very cramped view of what freedom really means. People need to be able to make meaningful choices and to have some power to carry out those choices if they are to be free. They must actually have some control over their lives in order to be free. The freedom to own property is not likely to guarantee every individual the power to make and carry out meaningful choices. It may for some, but it is highly unlikely to do so for all, which is what an ethic of freedom should be able to deliver.

What if the impoverished individual mentioned in the last paragraph is destitute because another set of individuals owns all the property in the area and refuses to let the penniless person have access to any of it? What if they refuse to hire this individual, hoard all the material goods in the area, and watch the needy person slowly die of malnutrition while they allow food and shelter to go to waste because they have much more than they themselves need? Is this really a picture of freedom?

A basic problem with libertarianism is that it conceives of human beings as not being social creatures. So, from this point of view, human beings have no obligations toward each other aside from those they assume when they form a contract binding them to certain obligations. Absent a contract, no obligations exist. This perspective certainly violates the Kantian perspective, which holds that each individual is owed the conditions necessary to obtain the freedom to choose and to develop his or her capacity to act freely. This would include respect for not only negative rights, but also positive rights necessary for self-development. A starving individual is hardly free to develop himself or herself. Therefore, Kant would find it legitimate that governments may impose taxes, impose limits on the use of property (like environmental regulations), and impose limits on contracts (such as minimum wage or anti-discrimination laws) when these actions are necessary for the welfare or self-development of those not able to support themselves otherwise.

Kantian Ethics: A Summary

Kantian ethics has a lot going for it. It seems to do a better job than utilitarianism does in accounting for individual rights and obligations we hold toward all individuals. It seems to be less prone to sacrifice the individual for the sake of the welfare of the greater society. But, it is not without its own problems. It can be very vague in providing guidance in many practical situations, and it may have a problem dealing with situations where rights seem to be in conflict. Despite these problems, Kant's ethical theory has had an enormous impact on modern thinking about morality.

Chapter Questions ———————————————————

1. What is a deontological ethical theory?

2. The local humane society has just called you to ask for a donation. You agree to give a very large donation but only if they include you in their press release to the local newspapers. According to Kant, is this an ethical action on your part? Why or why not?

3. What does Kant mean by universal rules?

4. What is Kant's categorical imperative? How does it differ from the golden rule?

5. Kant states that we must never use a person just for our own purposes. What does this mean? Give an example of how this can happen.

6. What are negative and positive rights? Give examples of each.

7. Is dishonesty ever considered a moral action according to Kant? Explain your answer.

8. What does Kant mean when he says that the rights of the individual must be protected against the will of the majority? Explain your answer.

9. How does libertarian theory differ from Kantian theory? Explain your answer.

10. Why is Milton Friedman considered a libertarian? Explain your answer.

Thinking Exercise

Apply a Kantian analysis to ethical issues that arose in a work situation you have experienced. Describe the circumstances. What was the specific problem and how did you handle it? Did your solution coincide with a Kantian solution? Explain your answer.

4

An Ethic of Justice:
Treating Others Fairly

"JUSTICE" is a word often used when making moral judgements. We believe in justice and oppose injustice, but what exactly do we mean by terms like "justice" and "injustice?" Usually, we think of justice as *being fair*. Justice requires that we treat everybody fairly.

What does it mean to treat everybody fairly? In the first place, it requires that we treat like cases alike. Justice is a *comparative* term: it involves comparing cases and making sure that we are not discriminating or treating people differently who are alike in relevant respects. To a certain degree, our notion of justice is based on the notion of individual rights. A violation of an individual's rights is considered an injustice. This is certainly part of our conception of justice, but not all of it.

Three Types of Justice

Aristotle, an ancient Greek philosopher (384–322 BC), divided the concept of justice into three types: 1) distributive justice, 2) retributive justice, and 3) compensatory justice. Distributive justice, perhaps the most basic kind, concerns the division of benefits and burdens among individuals. These must be distributed fairly. Retributive justice concerns what form of "retribution," or punishment, should be imposed on someone who has done wrong. When we say, "The punishment must fit the crime," we are calling for retributive justice. Finally, compensatory justice refers to what kind and amount of compensation someone should receive if he or she been wronged. Again, we tend to think that compensation should in some way be proportional to the degree of damage that has been done. The greater the wrong or the greater the damage, the greater should be the compensation.

Distributive Justice

Distributive justice requires that equals be treated as equals; like cases be treated alike. The tricky question is: in what respects are we equal, and in what respects are we unequal? No one argues that all people are exactly alike, or equal, in all respects. We all have multiple ways in which we are different: different looks, different genders, different heights, different personalities, etc. For many purposes, we might say that these differences are irrelevant—we share a sameness simply because we are all human beings. For other purposes, however, certain differences may be relevant, and discrimination on the basis of those differences is entirely permissible. For example, differences of skill are obviously relevant to the performance of many jobs. A hospitality or tourism employer is perfectly justified in discriminating against those without the needed skills by hiring only those who have the proper skills for the job.

There is a long history of disputes over what distributive justice (fairness) requires regarding the distribution of benefits and burdens. What principles should govern how we distribute these? One candidate is the principle of *equality,* and those who strongly advance this principle are known as *egalitarians.* Egalitarians start with the basic principle that burdens and benefits should be equally divided among all. The ideal of equality has obvious appeal. The U.S. Declaration of Independence states, "All men are created equal." Societies with highly unequal distributions of income and resources are often criticized for such an arrangement, which is thought to be unjust. Equality of treatment of all persons tends to be a general goal of virtually all societies (especially the advanced industrial ones).

Despite the popularity of equality, it has been criticized as an inadequate basis for distributing benefits and burdens. An important criticism argues that it would be unjust to force total equality on people who are different in so many ways— ways that the critics argue are relevant to distribution of wealth or other positive goods, like power. For example, does it make sense to give exactly the same income to someone who works twice as long as another person at the same job, accomplishing twice as much? Or, to reward equally the industrious person who works hard and the lazy person who refuses to work at all or who works very little? Or, to not give greater medical resources to the very sick individual than we give to the person who is perfectly healthy?

Most egalitarians agree that some inequalities of treatment are justified. But they would argue that, at the very least, every human being is entitled to a certain minimum of income needed to survive at a reasonable standard of living, irrespective of any differences used to justify inequalities. Those who put a lower priority on equality would dispute this claim, of course.

A number of bases for differential incomes have been suggested. One is differential payment according to *effort.* If payment is according to effort, the lazy person will not be rewarded equally with the hard working individual. In a society that believes in a strong work ethic, rewarding people according to their effort seems to make a lot of sense. However, reward according to effort runs into problems because it ignores the question of whether someone's efforts are actually producing anything of value. Should the person who tries very hard, but who produces next to nothing of any value, be highly rewarded? Most of us would say that effort alone is not enough: something of value must be produced by all that effort.

Another possibility would be payment according to *ability.* Those with greater abilities are likely to produce more of value. People with higher skills tend to be paid higher starting salaries, so there is no doubt that this criterion is used to some degree in the United States to determine compensation. However, some would argue that ability is a poor determinant of compensation because it does not necessarily translate into a greater contribution or a more meritorious claim on resources.

For some decisions, the criterion of *need* is used. This principle is built into most health insurance policies: the most needy draw the greatest medical resources, even if they have not put in the most through their insurance premium payments. Government assistance during disasters or assistance to those with disabilities or those unable to otherwise provide for themselves is often distributed according to principles based on need; the greater the need, the greater the assistance. On the other hand, private sector market relations ignore need almost entirely. An employee with a large family (and therefore great needs) does not get paid more than does a single individual doing the same work for the same employer but who has no family. A customer with greater needs generally does not get a discount price, etc.

Yet another possible criterion for determining payment is *productivity*. This is the standard that most private sector firms in a capitalist economy would claim they use to determine pay levels. A more productive employee is paid more; a less productive one less. This raises questions about how to measure productivity, especially in industries where the "product" is something like a service that cannot be easily reduced to "units." How does one measure the "productivity" of a research scientist, an entertainer, an athlete, etc.? Also, if we used only productivity to decide income, can we ignore need entirely and allow the disabled and the mentally handicapped and others to starve to death because of their minimal or nonexistent productivity?

It is apparent that different principles of distribution are used in different contexts. The family, for instance, does not distribute its resources according to productivity. Children and the elderly who contribute no economic wealth are taken care of according to the principle of need. In a market economy like capitalism, distribution is determined by some measure of productivity. In a socialist economy, the goal would be to distribute burdens and benefits according to the famous dictum of Karl Marx (1818–1883): from each according to his (or her) ability; to each according to his (or her) need. Government programs often distribute burdens and benefits according to a changing array of the above factors, depending on the purpose of the program.

Clearly, no one of the above principles (total equality, distribution according to effort, ability, need, productivity, etc.) seems to provide a comprehensive, overall criterion by which we can determine a just, or fair, distribution of burdens and benefits. What is needed is a theory that would be applicable in all cases, one that provides clear guidance as to what is ethical and just.

John Rawls: Justice as Fairness

John Rawls, a 20th Century American philosopher (1921–2002), developed a comprehensive theory of justice that attempts to cover all situations.[1] Rawls argues that the only way to determine what is just, or fair, is to determine what would be

---

[1] See John Rawls, "Justice as Fairness," *Philosophical Review* 67, no. 2 (April 1958): 164–194 and John Rawls, "Distributive Justice," in Peter Laslett and W. G. Runciman, eds., *Philosophy, Politics, and Society*, 3d series (New York: Barnes and Noble, 1967), pp. 58–82. See also John Rawls, *A Theory of Justice* (Cambridge, Mass.: Belknap Press, 1971). The final book, *A Theory of Justice*, is Rawls's most famous work.

accepted as fair by rational people who would consider all points of view. That is, people who could evaluate whether a particular arrangement or a particular action seems just—whether you are on the giving or receiving end, in the advantaged or disadvantaged position. If it seems just and fair from *all points of view,* it is. If it appears unfair from the point of view of the person who benefits least, it may be an unjust arrangement.

How can we actually look at things from the point of view of everyone? We all know our own position in society, so we will inevitably be looking at things from the point of view of what looks fair from our own perspective. To remedy this tendency to see things only from our own point of view, Rawls proposes the following arrangement: suppose people had to decide what are just and fair social arrangements, and they had to come to unanimous agreement on what those are. However, the people making the decision will not know which position they may end up occupying in that society. Will you be the hotel general manager? Or, will you be the room attendant? Will you be the restaurant cashier, the line cook, the executive chef, or the restaurant owner?

Each person may end up in the most favored or privileged position, but he or she may also end up in the least favored or most underprivileged position. Not knowing where they will end up (in a hotel setting it could be the general manager or the front desk agent or the room attendant, etc.), all persons will be forced to take the viewpoint of all the people in the society (or the hotel, restaurant, etc.).

According to Rawls, when people take this viewpoint, they will come up with a just, or fair, arrangement. They will do so because they will be concerned that their own interests are taken care of and the only way to ensure that is to consider equally everyone's interests and perspectives. From such a "universal" perspective, the agreements arrived at will be just and fair.

The "Original Position" and the "Veil of Ignorance"

Rawls calls the position of people who do not know where they will end up in the society the *original position*. Those in the original position are operating behind what he calls the *veil of ignorance*. The veil of ignorance means that people do not know whether they will end up being male or female, light-skin colored or dark-skin colored, more wealthy or less wealthy, able-bodied or disabled, young or old, more intelligent or less intelligent, more ambitious or less ambitious, highly skilled or less skilled, good looking or unattractive, a member of religion A or religion B, a supervisor or a laborer, etc. Thus, they will devise social arrangements (working conditions, for example) that do not discriminate unjustly (or unfairly) against any of these groups. They will set up the rules and social arrangements that make sure each of these categories of people (and any other categories) are treated equally, unless their difference is relevant to unequal treatment (and acknowledged by all to be relevant).

Notice that Rawls assumes that people in the *original position*, operating behind the veil of ignorance, do have a few characteristics. First, they are all rational—that is to say, they will not act irrationally and intentionally choose to adopt rules that violate their own beliefs and interests. Second, they are self-interested. That means they will try to avoid consequences that could harm themselves. They are interested in their own well-being and their own survival. They will also know enough about society and social arrangements to know what the consequences would be of setting up society according to any particular set of rules. But beyond that, they will not know what their own ultimate characteristics or interests will be, and this will keep them from adopting rules that are racist, sexist, or any other type of "ist" that discriminates in an irrelevant (and thus unjust) way against a group of people.

Strengths of Rawls's System

Rawls's system certainly seems like a fair or just way to set up the rules by which a society or organization should operate. The very process used to arrive at the results seems to ensure that justice will prevail. If Rawls's theory is correct, it provides an important addition to either utilitarianism or Kantian ethics. Recall that one of the main objections to utilitarianism is that it does not provide for a just distribution of benefits—it only pays attention to maximizing the total amount of benefits while possibly ignoring the justice or injustice of how they are distributed. And, while Kant provides for individual rights, he says very little directly about justice or fairness in distribution.

The Basic Principles of Justice

What kind of rules would people adopt if they were in the *original position*, operating behind the veil of ignorance? Rawls argues that they would be extremely careful to avoid discriminatory consequences because each person would know that he or she may end up being the one discriminated against. As an example, we could use the laws that existed in the southern United States before the civil rights laws were enacted. Would those laws have persisted had the lawmakers not known previously if they were to be black or white? Probably not. People in the *original position* would assume that their worst enemy was assigning them their final place in society or in the institution whose rules they are deciding.

What principles would people choose under these circumstances? Rawls states that they would choose two basic principles. The first, which has come to be known as the *principle of equal liberty,* states that: "each person engaged in an institution or affected by it has an equal right to the most extensive liberty compatible with a like liberty for all."[2] Rawls's second principle has two parts. It concerns the circumstances under which unequal treatment would be permitted. He argues that inequalities would only be allowed if:

(a) It is reasonable to expect that they will work out to everyone's advantage.

and

---

[2] John Rawls, "Distributive Justice". Quote taken from selection reprinted in Shari Collins-Chobarian, ed., *Ethical Challenges to Business as Usual* (Upper Saddle River, N.J.: Pearson Prentice Hall, 2005), p. 57.

(b) The positions and offices to which they attach or from which they may be gained are open to all.[3]

Rawls identifies principles (a) and (b) above as the *difference principle* and the *principle of fair equality of opportunity*. Each of these principles are explored in the sections that follow.

Principle of Equal Liberty

At a societal level, the principle of equal liberty means that the liberties of every citizen have to be protected equally, and cannot be infringed upon, even for the sake of greater overall social benefits. The basic liberties included here are such civil liberties as freedom of speech, freedom of religion, freedom from arbitrary arrest, freedom to hold personal property, and the like. Applied to businesses or corporations, this principle implies that it is unjust for a business to: invade the privacy of employees, use its political and economic clout to influence legislation, pressure or force managers to engage in a particular kind of political activity, etc. All of these would be an unjust denial of equal personal and political freedoms to others. Likewise, our equal freedom to form contracts with others would be denied if others used force, fraud, or deception in business practices, or if they refused to honor valid contracts. These practices are unethical and are a violation of the principle of equal liberty.[4]

Rawls argues that this principle of equal liberty would be chosen because everybody in the *original position* would want to protect his or her own civil, personal, and political liberties above all else. Therefore, this first principle takes priority over all others, since it is basic to all other processes that could lead to either just or unjust outcomes.

The Difference Principle

The difference principle requires that the inequality has to benefit the least advantaged as well as those who obviously benefit from the inequality. This means that *everyone* must benefit from the inequality, including the person being given less. How could that ever be the case? Perhaps a simple example will illustrate how this is possible.

Suppose some good or benefit is produced and distributed. Consider three possibilities of how this good could be distributed as shown in Exhibit 1.

Since utilitarianism aims for the greatest overall good, with little regard for how that good is distributed, Distribution A and Distribution B would be ethically identical from a utilitarian perspective. But from Rawls's perspective, A is clearly preferable to B, since the good is distributed more justly (fairly). This appears to be a clear difference between utilitarianism and a Rawlsian justice perspective.

---

[3] John Rawls, "Distributive Justice". Quote taken from selection reprinted in Shari Collins-Chobarian, ed., *Ethical Challenges to Business as Usual* (Upper Saddle River, N.J.: Pearson Prentice Hall, 2005), p. 57.

[4] John Rawls, *A Theory of Justice*, pp. 108–114 and 342–350.

Exhibit 1

Distribution A	Distribution B	Distribution C
Person 1 25	Person 1 30	Person 1 40
Person 2 25	Person 2 27	Person 2 28
Person 3 25	Person 3 23	Person 3 22
Person 4 25	Person 4 20	Person 4 12
TOTAL 100	100	102

The difference becomes even clearer when we consider Distribution C. Recall that utilitarianism aims for the greatest benefit for the greatest number. Since Distribution C produces more of the good (102 units), than either A or B, presumably it is the preferable arrangement from a utilitarian perspective. Yet, from a Rawlsian view of distributive justice, Distribution C cannot be justified. Not only is it worse than Distribution A, but it is also worse than Distribution B, because the least favored individual (Person 4) is being treated unjustly (he or she gets only 12 units of the good, compared to 25 or 20 under the other two arrangements.)

As a result, Rawls would say that Distribution A is ethically most justified, B is next best, and C is least justified. A utilitarian would say that C is ethically most justified, and A and B are morally equivalent since they each produce the same amount of good. Note that in picking A, Rawls is willing to sacrifice the most productive arrangement (Distribution C) because it unjustly distributes the good being produced and harms the least favored person (Person 4).

So far we have been considering situations where greater inequality ends up hurting the least advantaged person. In these situations, Rawls condemns the inequality as unjust. But it is possible that greater inequality could be to the advantage of even the least favored person. Consider the possibilities shown in Exhibit 2.

Exhibit 2

Distribution A	Distribution B	Distribution C	Distribution D
Person 1 25	Person 1 30	Person 1 40	Person 1 41
Person 2 25	Person 2 27	Person 2 28	Person 2 26
Person 3 25	Person 3 23	Person 3 22	Person 3 27
Person 4 25	Person 4 20	Person 4 12	Person 4 28
TOTAL 100	100	102	122

Distributions A, B, and C are the same as before. But, notice Distribution D. It is actually the *second most unequal* distribution of all four possibilities, since the difference between the least favored and the most favored is second largest (15 units). Differences are 0 for A, 10 for B, 28 for C, and 15 for D. Yet, despite this inequality, Rawls would endorse D as the ethically preferable situation, since the least advantaged (in this case, Person 2, even though it ended up being Person 4 in the other three examples), actually does better than the least advantaged in any of the other three situations. (The least favored gets 26 units, compared to 25, 20, and 12 in the other three examples.)

Therefore, Rawls's difference principle justifies inequalities, but only if the least advantaged person gains from the inequality. This is what people in the *original position* (behind the veil of ignorance) would choose, he states, because only this difference principle will protect them if they end up at the bottom of inequalities.

The difference principle extends well beyond simple distribution of whatever gets produced. It also applies to the broader practices of all major institutions in society. In the case of businesses, it asserts that business practices that harm the least advantaged are unethical. Since inefficiency and unproductive diversion of resources to those able to "corner" a market inevitably end up harming the least advantaged who are unable to monopolize markets, all anti-competitive practices such as price fixing and monopolization are unethical. So are environmentally degrading practices, since these practices again always end up costing our society's least advantaged citizens by diverting resources away from their needs to environmental cleanup. In addition, the poorest also tend to be the ones who end up most exposed to environmental hazards, again an injustice under the difference principle. So, polluting the environment for the sake of profit is unjust according to Rawls.

The Principle of Fair Equality of Opportunity

The principle of fair equality of opportunity states that everyone has to get an equal opportunity to obtain the most privileged positions and offices in society or in a just institution. This "equal opportunity" principle again makes sense to people in the *original position* operating behind the veil of ignorance. They want an equal chance at the best offered by society or the institution. They will not want to arbitrarily deny an opportunity to a particular group because they may turn out to be a member of that group.

The principle of fair equality of opportunity means that all forms of discrimination are unjust. But, it means more than just that. It also means that everyone must be provided the same opportunities to qualify for the best jobs and positions.

If the competition for good jobs can be compared to a competitive race, it is not enough to simply line everyone up at the same starting line and then claim that all had an equal opportunity to win. If some contestants have been given nutritious food and ample opportunity to train while others are denied the same, we cannot really say that they had an equal opportunity to win. Therefore, everybody must be given access to the training and education necessary to succeed in any competition for favored employment. Equal opportunity must mean equal treatment in all the prerequisites to success, so that any differences in outcome stem only from differences in ability or effort. This is a particularly important point for those who are poorest, because they frequently face numerous conditions in their lives that effectively deny them equal opportunities to rise to the top.

Criticisms of Rawls

Rawls's theory has won great acclaim and a great deal of attention from those who study ethical theories.[5] Despite widespread praise, Rawls has his critics, some of whom find his principles too "liberal" for their liking. Most of the criticism centers on the difference principle, which is seen as too friendly to the interests of the most disadvantaged people.

One criticism is that people in the *original position* (behind the veil of ignorance) would not choose the principles that Rawls claims they would. Some argue that people in the *original position* would choose to be much bigger risk-takers than Rawls allows. Perhaps they would choose much more unequal conditions that end up hurting those at the bottom, in the hope that they will be one of the lucky ones who end up in a favored position. If they are willing to take the risk, they might agree to quite unequal societies, far removed from the "welfare state" that Rawls claims is the only just society that those in the *original position* would pick. Utilitarians, for example, argue that people behind the veil of ignorance would really choose arrangements that maximize overall social welfare (that is, utilitarian arrangements), not necessarily those that protect the most disadvantaged.

Other critics attack the entire notion of a "veil of ignorance" and an "original position." They argue that such a position is not really possible, and that Rawls just ends up sneaking his own liberal and humanitarian principles behind the ignorance veil, thereby giving a false legitimacy to what are really just his own preferences. Some believe he displays a bias toward values specific to advanced industrial countries—people in underdeveloped countries would probably be happy to give up the liberties so precious to Rawls if they could gain greater material welfare, these critics argue. Others argue that the different liberties Rawls endorses may clash with each other, and he gives no basis for how to decide between them.

Readers will have to decide for themselves if any of these criticisms have merit. Whatever the criticisms, Rawls has exerted an enormous influence over the thinking of those concerned with ethics in the second half of the 20th Century.

Applying Rawls: An Illustration

Before leaving Rawls, let us examine a situation to illustrate his theory. Suppose a hotel chain is facing difficult economic times. The company's top executives have determined that they will have to cut back on their expenditures for pensions for the employees. How should the distribution of the size of the cutbacks be determined? For that matter, how should the size of pensions be determined in the first place?

---

[5] For some of the literature on Rawls's theory of justice, see Norman Daniels, ed., *Reading Rawls: Critical Studies on Rawls's "A Theory of Justice,"* (Stanford, Calif.: Stanford University Press, 1989); Samuel Freeman, ed., *The Cambridge Companion to Rawls* (New York: Cambridge University Press, 2002); and Robert Paul Wolff, ed., *Understanding Rawls* (Princeton, N.J.: Princeton University Press, 1977).

Rawls would argue that principles of justice require that the company treat its least advantaged employees no less favorably than they do the most advantaged, unless the differential treatment can be shown to actually benefit those at the bottom. On the face of it, this concept of justice challenges the practices of many employers, who may cut back, or even eliminate pension payments, for their lowest paid employees. At the same time they may leave untouched, or even increase, the pension payments for the top executives.

In this instance, it may be possible to argue that, in fact, the lowest paid employees actually benefit from this unequal treatment even though it increases inequality, because without it, the company would fold because the top executives would leave if they did not have pensions.

If, in fact, the top executives are indispensable and if they will indeed leave for greener pastures should they be required to share the burden with lower paid employees, this argument may be correct. However, all of these factual claims must be substantiated before this argument can be accepted, according to Rawls's theory of justice. Without proof that the "least" or the "lowest" benefit from the unequal treatment, such inequality cannot be justified. If taken seriously, this theory would force society and all of its institutions (including businesses) to examine and justify all aspects of any unequal treatment they practice.

Retributive Justice

Retributive justice addresses whether it is right to impose "retribution" (punishment) on someone who has done wrong, and, if a punishment is proper, what is the proper retribution, or penalty, that someone should pay for that wrong.

It is universally accepted that punishment can be justly meted out only after certain conditions have been met. First, it must be the case that persons who committed the wrong were aware of what they were doing, and that they freely chose to do it. A new line cook who lights a gas stove and accidentally damages restaurant property by doing what he or she normally does on the job cannot justly be punished if the damage happened because of a gas leak that was not within his or her area of responsibility. The cook may have started a fire or a minor explosion, but was not aware that he or she was causing a problem, and could not have reasonably been expected to know this. Or, if a cashier is forced to participate in an immoral act (stealing from the employer by handing over the day's proceeds) at gunpoint, they cannot be blamed and punished for wrongdoing. Thus, ignorance, or an inability to do otherwise, excuses one from responsibility. Punishment under such circumstances is unjust.

Second, the person must be aware (or should reasonably be expected to be aware) that what they are doing is wrong. People so retarded or mentally ill that they are unable to distinguish right from wrong are not morally responsible, and thus cannot be justly punished for their actions.

Third, the proof of guilt must be substantial. Imposing "collective guilt," and thereby punishing an entire group because you are unable to pinpoint exactly who is the guilty party, is completely unjust. Likewise, incomplete proof or flimsy evidence is not sufficient to impose punishment, and any attempt to impose penalties under these circumstances would be unjust. If sheets and towels are regularly found missing from the linen supply closet of a large hotel, it would be unjust to fire all of the housekeepers on that basis alone.

Finally, the type and severity of the punishment should be proportional to, or appropriate to, the wrong committed. This is the meaning of the familiar saying, "The punishment must fit the crime." More severe infractions merit more serious penalties, and lesser offenses deserve lighter penalties. Beyond that, punishment must be given out in a fair and impartial manner. If a hotel department manager is fired for sexually harassing employees, and then a department manager is also found to be sexually harassing employees, the department manager must also be fired, even if the hotel does not want to lose that department manager.

Like cases must be treated alike. A company cannot justly apply harsh penalties to some for a particular infraction while allowing other favored employees to get off with lighter penalties or no penalty for the same infraction. To do so would be a violation of the principles of retributive justice.

Compensatory Justice

Compensatory justice is concerned with the proper way to "make it up" to someone who has been wronged. In other words, what is the proper restitution for them? How should they be compensated for the wrong done to them?

A general rule is that the person who has harmed another should give them back what they have improperly taken from them. For example, if an investment advisor has bilked investors out of thousands of dollars, that advisor must pay them back all the money they lost. Or, if a person has been unjustly dismissed from his or her job, he or she should receive back pay along with reinstatement.

However, sometimes it is impossible to restore what has been lost. A person who was criminally assaulted on the street and lost the ability to walk cannot be restored the power to walk. In this case, perhaps they should be compensated with the "equivalent value" of their ability to walk. But, of course, it is very difficult, if not impossible, to put a value on something like one's ability to walk. Many other things are equally difficult to value in a monetary sense. For example, if I ruin the reputation of your restaurant by falsely claiming that I contracted food poisoning from food eaten there, how much is your restaurant's reputation worth?

There are a number of difficult problems like this in determining what constitutes proper compensation. However, the general rule seems to be that, to the degree possible, justice demands that people be "made whole." That is, that they be given back what they have lost or its equivalent.

By far the biggest controversies in recent times in the United States concerning justice and compensation have been about programs that grant preferential treatment to a group that has been unjustly discriminated against in the past. For example, if a racial group has been unjustly discriminated against in the past, and this injustice has resulted in many of its members occupying the lowest rungs of society's economic ladder, is it just to make up for this by giving preference to members of this racial group for education, training, and promotional opportunities?

Programs of this nature are usually referred to as "affirmative action" programs. Polls show that the term "affirmative action" is very emotionally laden. Simple use of the term immediately raises heated, vehement opinions. This makes it hard to look at the issue dispassionately; the debate over affirmative action has often generated more heat than light.

Nevertheless, there are important and difficult questions to be worked out in regard to this subject. Does preferential access violate justice by denying equal treatment? Or does it create the conditions for equal treatment, which otherwise would be impossible given a history of past discrimination?

There are a number of complex issues involved in this discussion, and we will not be able to address them here. Consider what each of the ethical theories we have covered in this and previous chapters would say about this issue. How would utilitarianism resolve it: what would produce the "greatest good for the greatest number?" How would Kantian ethics evaluate the issue: which perspective upholds the categorical imperative's demand that we treat each individual as an end-in-himself or end-in-herself? What about Rawls's theory of justice: which perspective fulfills the principle of liberty, the difference principle, and the principle of fair equality of opportunity?

Chapter Questions

1. What are the three types of justice according to Aristotle? Define each one.
2. Does justice require welfare payments to the most needy people? Explain your answer.
3. Does justice require a minimum wage be paid to all working people? Explain your answer.
4. According to Rawls, what is the *original position*?
5. According to Rawls, what is the *veil of ignorance*?
6. What is the "principle of equal liberty"? Give an example.
7. In business, the "difference principle" would protect the most disadvantaged person. What does this mean? Give an example and explain your answer.
8. Punishment is an example of what type of justice?
9. Restitution is an example of what type of justice?
10. Affirmative action falls within the realm of what type of justice? Explain your answer.

Thinking Exercise

Apply a justice analysis to ethical issues that arose in a work situation you have experienced. Describe the circumstances. What was the specific problem and how did you handle it? Did your solution coincide with a justice solution? Explain your answer.

5

Virtue Ethics:
Aristotle and the Good Life

THE ETHICAL THEORIES we have considered so far have been concerned with principles or rules to govern our actions. There is, however, another way to look at ethical issues. Instead of concerning ourselves with ethical or unethical actions, we can make ethical judgments about the people undertaking those actions. In this regard, we are judging their *character*, which is what the ethical school of thought known as "virtue ethics" does.

Judging Character

When we judge the morality of people's character as well as the morality of their actions, we are comparing what kind of person they are to what kind of person we believe they *should be*. If we say of someone, "He is evil. He is heartless and cruel." we are not judging his actions but, instead, what sort of person he is. The ethical school of thought known as "virtue ethics" is built around this type of judgment.

Virtue ethics claims that the main task of ethics is not to supply us with rules for what is the right type of action, or what is a "good" action. Rather, virtue ethics aims to reveal the right type of person—the "good" person. What kind of character must a person have to be a moral human being? By examining character rather than actions, virtue ethics does not contradict the theories we have previously studied; it simply offers a "different angle" into morality. Because a "good" person will engage in "good" actions, and because habitually engaging in good actions leads to the development of a good person of good character, virtue ethics offers a complementary way of looking at morality. It is a unique perspective, and it may well afford us additional insight into moral behavior.

Aristotle: A Virtuous Character

The most famous proponent of virtue ethics is Aristotle, the ancient Greek philosopher.[1] Aristotle claimed that good character could be discovered by learning if a person is morally "virtuous." For Aristotle, a morally virtuous person constantly and habitually acts the way a human being should. He or she displays the virtues

---

[1] See Aristotle, *Nicomachean Ethics*, trans. David Ross (Oxford University Press, 1998). The book was originally published in 350 B.C.

and avoids the many vices by which we are so frequently tempted. A lifetime of virtuous living and avoidance of vice forms a morally virtuous character.

For Aristotle, a moral virtue is the disposition or tendency to do the right thing and avoid doing wrong. We develop this disposition over time and through training. In other words, a good character is an achievement, not a natural endowment. "Doing right" becomes second nature to us, if we have developed our moral character properly. This is not something that is naturally bred into us; we must strive to achieve a virtuous character, and we do this by constantly practicing the virtues and thereby developing a good character.

The Golden Mean

What exactly is a moral virtue? How can we distinguish it from non-virtuous traits or characteristics? For Aristotle, moral virtues follow from our nature as human beings. Virtues enable human beings to act in accordance with our "essence" or human nature. For Aristotle, the feature that distinguishes humans from all other creatures is our *ability to reason*. Therefore, the virtues are those traits or characteristics that enable us to act according to reason. We must act in a reasonable fashion.

We act in a reasonable fashion and exercise reason when we choose to act in a way that goes neither to excess nor to deficiency. Excess and deficiency always designate a vice. The middle ground, neither going too far or not far enough, is where virtue lies. Thus, virtue is a *golden mean* between the vice of deficiency and the vice of excess. To quote Aristotle:

> Virtue then is a state of deliberate moral purpose consisting in a mean that is relative to ourselves, the mean being determined by reason, or as a prudent man would determine it. It is a mean state...lying between two vices, the vice of excess on the one hand, and vice of deficiency on the other. . .[2]

A person who leads a life of moderation, avoiding deficiencies and excesses, leads a virtuous life. This the best that human beings can be: live according to the virtuous middle path between the errors or vices of going too far or not far enough. As Aristotle would put it, such a person will engage in the right action, at the right time, in the right manner, with the right goal as determined by reason. This is a difficult achievement, for there is only one way to get it right, while there are many ways to get it wrong. Nevertheless, according to Aristotle, the person who is able to get it right will exhibit a virtuous character and lead a "happy," fulfilled life worthy of a human being.

Virtue Examples

All of this may seem rather abstract. Perhaps examples can make it clearer. Aristotle names many virtues, but the four fundamental moral ones are *courage*, *temperance*, *justice* and *prudence*. Courage is the *golden mean* between the vices of

---

[2] Aristotle, *Nicomachean Ethics*. Quote taken from selection reprinted in Shari Collins-Chobarian, ed., *Ethical Challenges to Business as Usual* (Upper Saddle River, N.J.: Pearson Prentice Hall, 2005), p.13.

cowardice (deficiency) and recklessness or foolhardiness (excess). A courageous person shows just the right amount of bravery and displays a virtuous character. The coward has too little bravery; a reckless individual has too much. Only reason can tell us what is exactly the right amount of bravery, and once it does, a person must practice and develop the virtue of courage so that acting courageously becomes habitual. For example, if you knew that wrongdoing, such as fraud, was widespread at your place of work, would you be brave enough to report it? Would you be brave enough even if you knew some of your friends would be very angry with you for making the report?

Regarding the desire for food and other bodily pleasures, the virtue is temperance. Temperance is the *golden mean* between gluttony (excess) and extreme self-denial, sometimes called asceticism or austerity (deficiency). A virtuous man or woman, according to Aristotle, will neither over-indulge nor deny himself or herself the bodily pleasures that come from things like good food and drink. Missing the mark and going to either excess or self-denial makes one a less happy or less fulfilled human being. Both lead to a less virtuous life. For instance, do you know when to stop filling up your plate when you are dining at the local buffet restaurant? Or, do you know when to stop drinking when you are at a party?

Justice is the virtue of giving other people exactly what they deserve, neither more nor less. It is the *golden mean* between two forms of injustice: either giving them less than they deserve, or giving them more than they deserve. We covered justice in the previous chapter, so it should be apparent that the task of treating others justly is a complicated task. Aristotle would say that only reason can tell us what is just, and only constant practice in treating others justly can build a virtuous character, so that we habitually treat others in a just manner.

Prudence, or wisdom, is the virtue that helps us to know what is reasonable in different situations. It is an extremely important virtue, because it enables us to avoid excess and deficiency in other areas, and thus is fundamental to avoiding a life of vice and immorality. Only a prudent or wise person will know how to avoid extremes. Imprudence is the vice in opposition to prudence, and it can err in both directions. It is possible to imprudently or unwisely over-do (or under-do) virtually any action, emotion, or desire. An imprudent or unwise person then becomes a slave to his or her emotions or desires and misses the mark of moderation, thereby living a life of vice. For example, do you know people who fluctuate wildly in their enthusiasms, going from one extreme to another, without ever seeming to find a steady set of interests or goals? According to Aristotle, such a faddish person lacks the virtue of prudence or wisdom.

There are numerous other virtues that could be mentioned, although the four mentioned above are the most central ones to Aristotle. Additional moral virtues include: trustworthiness, honesty, generosity, civility, sincerity, gentleness, reliability, warmth, dependability, cooperativeness, empathy, tact, kindness, tolerance, benevolence, etc.

The Relationship of Virtues to Moral Principles

In many ways, virtue ethics is closely related to the rules and principles presented earlier, because a person acting on the basis of the various virtues will, in some ways, behave according to those rules and principles. For example, the virtues of generosity and kindness are fully congruent with utilitarianism. A disposition to act generously and kindly will lead one to maximize benefits for others and minimize their pains and sorrows. Likewise, the virtues of honesty, trustworthiness, justice, and sincerity are fully compatible with Kant's insistence on always treating another human being as an end-in-himself or end-in-herself and to never degrade them to the level of a "thing." And certainly, the virtue of justice is directly related to principles of justice, no matter how they may be discovered and applied. So, virtue ethics should not be thought of as necessarily in conflict with the three theories we covered earlier. Of course, it may not be completely in accord with any or all of them, either; it depends on how the virtues are understood and applied in actual practice.

The Relationship of Virtues to "Human Nature"

A virtuous person is one who totally fulfills what it means to be a complete human being; those who are less virtuous are less successful at being fully human. This means that one's idea of virtue depends on one's idea of human nature and the purpose of life.

For example, St. Thomas Aquinas, the Christian philosopher in the Middle Ages who became the most important philosopher of the Roman Catholic Church, adopted Aristotle's ethical theory virtually in its entirety. Aquinas agreed with Aristotle that the four fundamental virtues are courage, temperance, justice, and prudence. However, as a Christian, Aquinas felt that the purpose of life was not merely to live according to reason in this life, but to unite with God in a future life. Therefore, Aquinas added three specifically Christian virtues: faith, hope, and charity. These virtues made sense to Aquinas but they would not have made sense to Aristotle, who was not a Christian and did not believe in an afterlife. Thus, the virtues for different followers of this school of thought are not always identical—they will vary according to the view of humanity and purpose of human life held by the particular theorist.

In some cases, the different conceptions of humanity can lead to opposite views of what constitutes a virtue and what constitutes a vice. Aquinas, for example, held that humility is a virtue and pride is a vice, because these views fit with his Christian beliefs and the teachings of his sacred texts. Aristotle, coming from an aristocratic Greek society, felt that pride is a virtue and humility is a vice. Thus, virtue ethics presupposes agreement on some fundamental issues about the nature and purpose of human life. Without that agreement, there will likely be disagreement concerning what are virtues and what are vices.

Despite these differences, there is rather widespread agreement across many differing cultures and religions on a number of basic virtues and vices. Virtually no one, for instance, finds cruelty, arrogance, injustice, cowardice, self-centeredness, dishonesty, insensitivity, etc., to be virtues.

Criticisms of Virtue Ethics

As with all the other theories, virtue ethics has a number of critics. One criticism flows directly from points made earlier. Critics charge that virtue ethics is so dependent on one particular worldview that it is not much use in a multicultural world with a variety of religions and traditions. It is not a usable ethic for all of us, charge these critics—only for those willing to accept a particular understanding of "human nature" and of the role of humans in this world.

Supporters of virtue ethics could answer this charge in a variety of ways. First, it could be argued that there may be differences at the margins, but in some very fundamental ways, we all see certain characteristics as virtuous no matter what cultural background or religious tradition we come from. These "universal" virtues (like justice and honesty and courage and others) provide a very good foundation for judging people's character. Also, the virtues that may be specific to a particular group (such as Aquinas's Christian virtues of faith, hope, and charity) are still useful moral "anchors," or reference points, for members of that group, even if a society has decided not to impose those particular values on all of its members. As long as the appropriate values and virtues are applied to the appropriate group (one holding to those values as a basis of social cohesion), there is no fundamental clash between virtue ethics and a multicultural and multireligious world.

A second criticism is that virtue ethics is not really very useful because it fails to give us any practical guidance on how we should actually behave when we are faced with difficult circumstances. Critics argue that it is all well and good to admonish people to build their character through virtuous practice, but that does not help much in a genuinely perplexing moral dilemma. For example, suppose a company manager is facing an agonizing decision about whether to fire a loyal, earnest employee who is, at best, marginally competent and definitely not as productive as all others working in her position. Does it help to tell this manager to build his character by practicing a virtuous life?

A defender of virtue ethics would reply that sound guidance can be obtained, even if the route to such guidance seems to be a bit indirect. The morality of an action depends on how it impacts a person's character. Those actions that create a morally virtuous (good) character are ethical or moral; those that create a morally vicious character are not. True, this principle does not create a simple set of rules to live by, but that is one of its strengths, not a weakness. Any simple set of rules that says "Do this. Don't do that." is bound to be too simplistic to fit all occasions. Wrestling with perplexing moral dilemmas is hard work, but so is developing a virtuous moral character. According to this defense of virtue ethics, the request for simple guidance in morally difficult circumstances is a demand for simplicity where no such "easy way out" is possible.

Many followers of virtue ethics argue that moral "dilemmas" are actually artificial creations that a person of good moral character is unlikely to ever encounter. These dilemmas are products of previous poor choices made by a less-than-virtuous person who has gotten himself or herself into such a problematic situation that there is no good way out. A person of good moral character who practices virtuous behavior would never get in such a fix in the first place, they assert. Therefore, the best practical advice is to practice the virtues and lead a morally virtuous life. Doing so will resolve a number of the seemingly insoluble "moral dilemmas," because those dilemmas never come up in the first place—if you lead the right kind of life.

Virtue Ethics and Social Institutions

Those who support virtue ethics assert that the theory can be just as helpful in evaluating our social arrangements and institutions as are utilitarianism, Kantian ethics, and justice ethics. Those institutions or practices that create people of bad moral character are to be condemned, while those that lead people to develop a good moral character are to be praised. For example, a social institution or system that teaches people to be greedy is immoral and should be criticized and changed. The same is true for a social arrangement that encourages laziness or dishonesty. To the follower of virtue ethics, this type of evaluation is just as concrete, practical, and useful as the guidance offered by the utilitarian "greatest happiness" rule, or the Kantian categorical imperative, or the Rawlsian principles of justice.

Applied to social institutions like businesses, Aristotelian virtue ethics would emphasize their character as human communities. Since many of the virtues have to do with our ability to live comfortably together in a community, a corporation or business would be judged by how well it contributes to the development of character (such as integrity, honesty, tolerance, fairness, and cooperation) of its employees and shareholders. Businesses or corporations that fail this test would be judged morally deficient. A corporate culture that emphasizes or encourages dishonesty, intolerance, greed, or deception would definitely be found wanting by this criterion. Numerous other examples could be given. For instance, there are many telemarketing firms that sell vacations that do not deliver on what they promise. These companies would be found ethically deficient according to virtue ethics.

The main point is that virtue ethics requires businesses to further the more social virtues relating to the ways we interact with each other in the community. Virtue ethics is not an ethical viewpoint concerned with isolated individuals; many of the virtues are inherently social in nature, and these are the virtues that will figure most prominently in ethical evaluations of businesses and corporations.

Chapter Questions

1. Define virtue ethics.
2. Who was the first proponent of virtue ethics?
3. What are the four fundamental moral virtues according to Aristotle? Define each one.
4. How would you critique virtue ethics?

Thinking Exercise

Apply a virtue ethics analysis to ethical issues that arose in a work situation you have experienced. Describe the circumstances. What was the specific problem and how did you handle it? Did your solution coincide with a virtue ethics solution? Explain your answer.

6

Applying Ethics to the Purchasing, Marketing and Sales Functions

"As economic inequalities have deepened during the last several decades, the renewed worship of money has bred temptation at all levels. Executives at Enron, WorldCom and other corporations, intoxicated by the heady atmosphere of deregulation, defraud shareholders of billions and get away with little or no punishment. The little guy naturally says: If the big shots get away with it, why not me? So he cheats on his taxes, steals from his company and downloads music without paying for it."[1]

MONEY can be a very powerful motivator to engage in unethical behavior. In a society obsessed with wealth, we all need to be aware of this danger. The purchasing, marketing and sales functions are monetary functions and any time money is involved, there is an opportunity for unethical behavior. People working in these areas need to examine their principles on a regular basis because of the potential ethical issues that can arise.

For example, consider the temptation to enrich yourself in a manner that is harmful, unfair, deceptive, etc., to the organization for which you work. When the temptation arises, analyze the situation by asking yourself, *"Is this the best decision for the organization that I work for?"* Beyond your own organization you must also ask, *"Is this the right decision for everyone involved?"* Self-enrichment at your employer's expense, if it is done without the employer's knowledge, will inevitably be a violation of a number of the ethical principles we have covered earlier. It will almost always turn out to be harmful to the greater good; it will also violate the rights of others and lead to unjust outcomes. Don't rationalize unethical behavior by thinking, *"Even if this is not the best organizational decision, it's not so bad and it would really help me out a lot."* If your actions in some way pilfer from your employer for your own gain, your behavior is unethical and rationalizations of that behavior will not withstand an honest ethical scrutiny.

If your organization, in an effort to achieve its own best advantage, should require you to engage in conduct that principled reasoning tells you is unethical, you will have to do the right thing—*even if it puts you at odds with your employer.*

---

[1] Jackson Leers, "Cheater, Cheater," *In These Times*, June 21, 2004, p. 28.

Consider the following example in which an employer attempts to protect his financial self-interest by pressuring an employee to stretch ethical boundaries.

You are working on a farm in Wyoming for the summer. Part of your job is to bring the cows in from the field in the evening. Last night, you saw two "downers" (animals that are unable to stand) when you went out to the field. You know from your food safety course that this could mean big trouble in the form of Mad Cow Disease. You immediately go to your boss who tells you that the animals are "just tired" and that he will "handle the situation." He also tells you not to mention the down cows to anyone.

The employer's decision to gloss over such a potentially dangerous situation is unconscionable. In a case such as this, an ethical person would find himself or herself at odds with the employer. The cows should be tested for Mad Cow Disease; if they are not tested, an outbreak could occur. You would be putting innocent people at risk of contracting the fatal brain-wasting condition known as Creutzfeldt-Jakob disease, which comes from eating meat infected with Mad Cow Disease.

Even after you have decided that something must be done to ensure that no one is exposed to the risk of contracting this horrendous disease, there are further ethical issues you must resolve. What exactly should you do? Handling this situation in a manner that is both ethically principled and practical will require a great deal of thought and soul-searching. Analyzing the issues with the help of the different philosophical theories presented earlier should help a great deal.

The rest of this chapter models the kind of analyses you can take to a variety of ethical situations that arise in relation to purchasing, marketing, and sales functions. The case below, "A Trip to Las Vegas," is followed by detailed ethical analyses in relation to each of the ethical theories presented earlier: utilitarianism, Kant's categorical imperative, Rawls's justice ethics, and Aristotle's ethics of virtue. The chapter closes with a series of case studies and questions about the cases that challenge you to analyze ethical issues in areas of purchasing, marketing, and sales.

Case Study—A Trip to Las Vegas

Mr. Brent Wiggly is the Director of Purchasing for the Commander Hotel Company, which owns and operates 78 hotels in the western United States. The average Commander Hotel has 200 rooms and suites. Mr. Wiggly purchases linens to service over 15,000 rooms.

Yesterday, Mr. Tom Penney, one of the top salespersons for the Linens of Today Company, arrived for his quarterly sales visit. He was very excited because he had a new product to offer, king sized bed sheets with a 200-cotton thread count for only $8.00 apiece.

Mr. Wiggly treated Mr. Penney in his typically cordial manner. However, at the end of the visit, Mr. Wiggly said, "I'm sorry Tom but I am making my next big purchase of sheets with the Advantage Linen Supply Company. A salesman was in here just two days ago. He offered me the exact product you have, but the cost to me would only be $7.90 per sheet. That would be a loss to the Commander Hotel Company of over $1,500, if I bought only one sheet per room."

> *"But, that's not all I have for you,"* Mr. Penney countered. He
> *pulled a rather large envelope out of his inside suit coat pocket and
> handed it to Mr. Wiggly. "It's an all-expenses paid vacation for two
> in Las Vegas. It includes airfare, hotel, and two meals a day,"* he
> *proudly declared.*
>
> *Mr. Wiggly opened the envelope. He couldn't believe his eyes.
> The tickets and the reservations were all there. "Wow,"* he thought to
> *himself. "My wife would sure love this! And what's an extra $1,500
> to the Commander Hotel chain anyway?"*

Mr. Wiggly may be absolutely correct in assuming that $1,500 would not mean much to his company. But what would happen if all of the managers felt that way? What would happen if each and every manager in the Commander Hotel chain spent $1,500 unnecessarily?

Anything that could be considered a bribe or kickback is a conflict of interest and, therefore, is unethical. It does not matter what form it takes. Different types of kickbacks include gifts, entertainment, and discounts on personal items from vendors. Another subtle form of kickback is when a person has influence or power within an organization and uses it inappropriately. For example, if your cousin Joe owns a Web-hosting firm and you hire him to design the company's Web site—this could be construed as a conflict of interest. However, if there is bidding for the contract and Joe's firm wins the bid honestly, this should be morally acceptable. In instances such as this, it is advisable for you to exclude yourself from the purchasing process.[2]

The moral basis of business relationships involves trust. Let's look at this in a methodical manner from the point of view of the various philosophers we studied earlier.

Case Commentary: Utilitarianism

From an act utilitarian perspective, we can ask which action brings the greatest good for the greatest number of people? It may seem simple at first: two people will have a wonderful vacation and one person will make a large sale and pocket a good-sized commission. Those would seem to be the pluses, if Mr. Wiggly were to accept the Las Vegas trip and to purchase linens from Mr. Penney. However, there are many others who will also be affected by the decision that Mr. Wiggly makes.

Act utilitarianism tells us to look at the consequences for everyone. The principled person will ask, *"What about the other people who work for the company? How is this decision affecting all of the employees in the Commander Hotel Company?"* Should all of the employees subsidize a vacation for Mr. Wiggly, the Purchasing Director? On a local basis, just at that chain property, $1,500 might have been earmarked for something to benefit other employees such as improvements to employee facilities or benefits. The employees may have to collectively "pay" for

---

[2] Linda K. Treviño and Katherine A. Nelson, *Managing Business Ethics: Straight Talk About How to Do It Right*, 3d ed. (Hoboken, N.J.:. Wiley, 2004), pp. 68–69.

Mr. Wiggly's vacation out of something they would otherwise have received. And they would "pay" for this without their knowledge or consent. If all of the consequences are considered, it is apparent that more harm is done than good.

Another negative impact of these types of actions is lower morale among the employees in the operation. If employees learn that others are getting away with accepting the bribes, an atmosphere of discontent would flourish. Employees would begin to think, *"If they can get away with it, so should I."* The workplace would become a breeding ground of demoralization.

A utilitarian would ask, *"What are all of the consequences of my actions?"* What about guests? Suppose that $1,500 was intended for new carpeting in an area where the old carpeting is torn and where recently several guests had tripped over the larger rips. What about the shareholders? The shareholders would undoubtedly lose money if actions such as Mr. Wiggly's went unchecked. The shareholders would sustain a loss of income and they would own a less valuable company. In addition, a glimpse at the long-term costs would certainly show us a less efficient organization. Eventually, this would lead to higher costs for consumers. Or, the hotel management may choose to lay off employees to cover the extra "overhead" costs. In any case, when dollars are spent for unbudgeted expenses, properties run less efficiently and less profitably.

A rule utilitarian would ask, *"What if everyone operated this way? What if everyone in the organization considered it suitable to accept bribes?"* The organization would run less profitably if all the managers wangled something extra for themselves at the expense of the company. If managers overspent their budgets while hiding the true causes ("perks" for themselves), each thinking they were the only one doing it, the bottom line would certainly suffer. This would translate into negative consequences for all stakeholders: employees, customers, owners, etc. Rules condoning universal bribery as a way of doing business could never be seen as promoting the greatest good for the greatest number.

The ethical individual must take this analysis even further. Let's look at this in terms of society as a whole. If we do so, it becomes apparent that a civilization that condones the universal taking of bribes makes for a much less satisfying and productive society. Just think what your day would be like if you had to bribe everyone from whom you asked something. What if you had to bribe your librarian for the book you need, or if you had to bribe your mailperson to deliver your mail? Such a world would not only be difficult to negotiate in, but it would breed widespread mistrust and cynicism as well. The consequences are deeply corrosive. In fact, it is difficult to believe that anyone would prefer a world of universal bribery to one without such practices. Therefore, if we are unable to make bribery a universal rule, we could not accept it as an ethical action. A rule utilitarian would say we could accept this type of action only if it was true that a rule stating everyone could do it would lead to the greatest benefit.

Case Commentary: Kant's Categorical Imperative ————

Kant states that the consequences of your actions are not the basis for making a moral decision. Instead, he argues that actions are moral or immoral based solely on their nature. If someone acts out of a sense of duty, because they know it is "the right thing to do," then that action is moral. We know the right thing to do by following the categorical imperative. The categorical imperative is the rule, or command, that we all must follow at all times in all places under all circumstances if we wish to act morally.

In the case of Mr. Wiggly and Mr. Penney, Kant would be hard pressed to find anything moral about the decision to accept the vacation. If Mr. Wiggly accepts the vacation he is doing it simply for the enjoyment both he and his wife will receive. He is not accepting it in an attempt to do his moral duty, but rather he is accepting it because it provides positive benefits for both himself and his wife.

From Kant's perspective, what is Mr. Wiggly's moral duty? What is the most rational decision? How should Mr. Wiggly think this through from a Kantian perspective?

The first step for Mr. Wiggly would be to try to universalize his decision. This means Mr. Wiggly would have to be able to say that his decision to accept the vacation would be a suitable decision for all of the managers and employees of the Commander Hotel Company. If he were to decide that the decision is suitable, then, according to Kant, his decision to accept the vacation could be relayed to all of the other managers and employees of the Commander Hotel Company. Conversely, if Mr. Wiggly is unable to universalize his decision then the decision must be immoral.

Bear in mind that Kant's first statement of the categorical imperative says that we must be able to make the rule or principle we are following into a universal rule. If that is not possible without being self-contradictory, the action is immoral. Could we make secret bribe-taking a universal rule without contradicting the entire basis of open, straightforward business transactions? We cannot; universal bribe-taking would completely undermine business transactions. It is therefore self-contradictory and immoral to engage in a business operation of any sort and take a bribe. Were he to accept the bribe, Mr. Wiggly would be acting immorally, since the other employees and managers would not be receiving the same freedom (to accept bribes) as he is granting to himself. That means he is violating the categorical imperative, that is, he is acting immorally.

Kant's second formulation of the categorical imperative also condemns deceptive practices like bribery. Whenever you engage in deception in business, you are treating other human beings merely as the means to your private ends, not as ends-in-themselves. You are not granting them the same status you claim for yourself—an autonomous, rational human being free to make decisions according to reason. By withholding information, or deceiving others, you degrade them to the status of a "thing" to be "used" (perhaps used to make money), and deny them their humanity. This is immoral, and Kant would say that all deceptive and/or dishonest business behavior is immoral. Lying, cheating, bribe-taking, deceiving, and so forth will always mean degrading your fellow human beings—violating the categorical imperative. According to Kant, you must never use a person just for your own purposes. Instead, you must treat every human being as someone of independent moral worth, with an equal claim to freely decide his or her own life choices.

One indication that we all implicitly accept Kant's point is that we feel the need to hide activities such as deception, cheating, taking bribes, etc. If we felt these were moral and acceptable actions, we would not act in a manner that is not "above board." If you have to hide it from your fellow employees, your employer, customers, etc., this is a "red flag" that the action is probably immoral according to Kant.

Case Commentary: The Ethic of Justice

John Rawls, the 20th Century American philosopher, contends that in order to determine what is fair, rational people must decide what would be accepted as reasonable from all points of view. He contends that people are expected to be self-interested but they also must consider the issues as if they do not know where they will alight in society. In other words, if you are part of a group making rules for a corporation, you must suggest rules that you would want followed whether you were the lowest paid clerk or the chief executive officer. If the corporation is deciding on contributions towards retirement funds, should the clerks receive less than the executives? If you did not know what position you would hold in the corporation (*the veil of ignorance*) you would ensure that everyone received a contribution that seemed fair in order to ensure your fair share.

Consider Mr. Wiggly in our "Trip to Las Vegas" case. To act justly, he would have to behave according to rules that would seem fair to him—no matter what his position within the Commander Hotel Company. What would the rules be if those who established them had no idea what their ultimate post at the Commander Hotel Company would be? Would the rules condone bribery? Would those who are not in the position of Purchasing Director accept rules giving the person in that position the freedom to accept bribes, or "gratuities" like a trip to Las Vegas, in exchange for purchase orders that harm the corporation—even if it is only a slight harm? Would they accept this as a just or fair set of rules? Where do we draw the line?

To even ask the question is to answer it. Rules allowing such behavior would result in numerous injustices. Bribery, according to Rawls, is contrary to the *principle of equal liberty*, which states that each person engaged in an institution or affected by it has an equal right to the most extensive liberty compatible with a like liberty for all.

Applied to businesses or corporations, this principle implies that it is both unfair and unwarranted for a business to engage in bribery in any form. However, the business ethics writer, John Boatright, contends that it is not necessarily a conflict of interest if a purchasing agent accepts a gift from a supplier who expects special treatment. He further claims that it depends on the value of the gift, the circumstances, as well as industry practice, and whether or not the gift violates any laws.[3] Boatright's position is an illustration of the differences of opinion that exist about issues like this in the hospitality industry as well as in other industries.

---

[3] John R. Boatright, *Ethics and the Conduct of Business*, 4th ed. (Upper Saddle River, N.J.: Prentice Hall, 2003), p. 144.

Nonetheless, according to Rawls, it would be unjustifiable for Mr. Wiggly to accept the bribe because his deceptive practices deprive numerous other people (fellow employees, company stockholders, customers) of liberty equal to that liberty he is claiming for himself. And he is accepting the bribe solely for his own personal gain.

Case Commentary: Aristotle and the Ethics of Virtue

With Aristotle's ethics of virtue, we judge a person's character. We look at the type of person he or she is to make our judgment. What is Mr. Wiggly's character if he accepts the bribe? Would he be acting in a virtuous manner?

Of the many character virtues, there are a few examples that are relevant to this case. Among Aristotle's four main virtues, the virtue of justice applies most directly here. Mr. Penney is committing an injustice by offering Mr. Wiggly more wealth than he is legitimately entitled to. And, if he should accept the bribe, Mr. Wiggly would be acting unjustly by accepting money (or its equivalent in a free vacation) to which he is not entitled. Both men would be committing an injustice by deceptively diverting resources into their own pockets and away from those to whom they should belong. We would therefore judge them to have a faulty character because they lack the virtue of justice and practice the vice of injustice.

Additionally, the deceitfulness involved in the entire transaction shows that both men have a dishonest character. This is a serious flaw, showing that they lack the virtue of honesty. From Aristotle's perspective, Mr. Wiggly would deserve severe condemnation if he accepts the free vacation. He would have a "bad" character, full of vice and lacking in important virtuous traits.

Ethical tradition also condemns this type of behavior. Many people turn to religion as their basis for ethical tradition. Religions worldwide are full of examples of the value of honesty in one's business dealings.

Honesty in your business dealings is a continual theme throughout both the Old and New Testaments. In Judaism, on the Yom Kippur holiday, which is the holiest day of the year for those of Jewish faith, readings from the Book of Leviticus are integrated into the service. An excerpt from the readings is, *"You must not steal; you must not act deceitfully nor lie to one another."* Also included is a statement on truthfulness regarding measurements, *"Do not pervert justice when you measure length, weight or quantity. You must have honest scales, honest weights, honest dry and liquid measures."*[4] Additionally, the Babylonian Talmud contends that the heavenly court for final judgment asks, *"Did you conduct your business affairs honestly?"*[5]

Christianity also includes many references to honesty in the New Testament. In Ephesians 4:25, it says, *"Put away falsehood; let everyone speak the truth with his neighbor, for we are members one of another."* In Matthew 7:12, it states, *"Therefore all*

---

4 Lev. 19:11.

5 Quoted in Grant Perry, "The Good Jew who went to Jail," *Reform Judaism* (Winter 2002): 26.

things whatsoever ye would that men should do to you, do ye even so to them,"[6] which is another way of saying, "Do to others as you would have them do to you."

Examples from Islamic culture are also numerous. The following quote is from the Koran: *"And give full measure when you measure out, and weigh with a true balance; this is fair and better in the end."*

It is evident from just these examples (see Exhibit 1 for more examples) that ethical traditions worldwide condemn this type of behavior. Within most religious traditions, there is nothing debatable about this type of behavior. This case fails ethical tests within all traditions.

Exhibit 1: Examples of Honesty Cited in World Scripture[7]

Let your conduct be marked by truthfulness in word, deed, and thought.	Hinduism. Taittiriya Upanishad 1.11.1
Be honest like Heaven in conducting your affairs	Taoism. Tract of the Quiet Way
Straightforwardness and honesty in the activities of one's body, speech, and mind lead to an auspicious path.	Jainism. Tattvarthasutra 6.23
He who utters gentle, instructive, true words, who by his speech gives offense to none—him I call a brahmana.	Buddhism. Dhammapada 406
Master Tseng said, "Every day I examine myself... In intercourse with my friends, have I always been true to my word?"	Confucianism. Analects 1.3

Conclusion

The desire for money can be very powerful. It can be so potent that it may distort our perspective and lead us to rationalize unethical behaviors as long as it makes us richer. Some people will do almost anything for money. Within the hospitality industry, it is necessary to develop oversight procedures to ensure that self-gain does not override common ethical decency. Even in a highly competitive environment, ethical standards must be maintained. The more competitive the environment, the more care must be taken to ensure that ethical standards are followed.

There have been various attempts at a "transcultural corporate ethic"[8] as a result of intergovernmental agreements over the last fifty years. Guidelines for business conduct for multinational corporations in areas such as employment poli-

---

6 Eph. 4:25, Matt. 7:12.

7 Andrew Wilson, ed., *World Scripture: A Comparative Anthology of Sacred Texts* (New York: International Religious Foundation, 1991).

8 W.C. Frederick, "The Moral Authority of Transnational Corporate Codes," *Journal of Business Ethics* 10: 165–177.

cies, consumer protection, environmental protection, political payments and basic human rights have been included.[9] There are four basic principles involved, one of which is market integrity in business transactions. This includes restrictions on political payments and bribes. The reasoning behind this is that bribes "inject non-market considerations into business transactions."[10]

Case Study—Spilled Coffee

Andy is the owner and manager of Global Coffee House, which offers a selection of coffees from around the world. Andy prides himself on the unique selections and blends of coffee that his store offers. He also takes great satisfaction in the comfortable surroundings of his shop.

For the last week, Andy has been very busy trying to finalize the offers he received to refurbish the coffee house for his technologically savvy customers by introducing wireless Internet service. Andy was in and out of his office all week meeting with suppliers and left all operations in the hands of his assistant, John. Andy felt sure that John would be able to do the job in his absence.

During one of his meetings, Andy received an alarming phone call from John. It appeared that Nancy, one of his regular customers, had to be taken to the emergency room at a nearby hospital. As she was picking up her coffee cup, the lid popped off and most of the very hot coffee spilled onto her arm. Andy got the name of the hospital from John and rushed immediately to the emergency room to look for Nancy and offer an apology.

On his way to the hospital, Andy started thinking about what might have led to this incident. The first thing that came to his mind was that a couple of weeks ago he changed his hot cup and lid purveyor to another company in order to cut costs and come up with extra cash to help pay for the Internet service refurbishment. He was not able to think of anything else that might have caused this problem.

Finally, Andy arrived at the hospital emergency room where he found Nancy, her arm covered with a bandage. Andy asked as politely as possible about what had happened. Nancy told him that just as she was reaching for her cup from John, the lid suddenly popped open and the hot coffee spilled onto her arm. The doctors told her that she is suffering from first-degree burns. Andy offered his sincere apology and promised to help in any way possible.

Andy returned to the coffee house. John was waiting for him. They sat down to discuss the situation. John told Andy that the new coffee cups are not the same quality as the ones they had previously. John demonstrated this by taking an empty cup with the lid on. He squeezed it just a bit and as he did, the lid popped off.

Andy was devastated about his cost saving decision. It was apparent to him that his poor judgment had led to the problem as well as to Nancy's burns.

9 Linda K. Treviño and Katherine A. Nelson, *Managing Business Ethics: Straight Talk About How to Do It Right*, 3d ed. (Hoboken, N.J.: Wiley, 2004), p. 43

10 W.C. Frederick, "The Moral Authority of Transnational Corporate Codes," *Journal of Business Ethics* 10: 165–177.

However, he also knew that he had thousands of cups and lids in his storeroom as well as a binding contract with the new purveyor.

Case Questions

1. What would you do in Andy's place?

2. What are the ethical issues involved in this case?

3. Would any of the philosophers tell Andy to keep the cups?

4. Would an act utilitarian's decision regarding this case be different from a rule utilitarian's decision? If so, how? Specify what those decisions would be.

This case was authored by Samer Hassan, Ph.D., Associate Professor of Hospitality Management at Johnson & Wales University, Florida Campus.

Case Study—The Board of Directors

Fairview Country Club is a private club with 265 affluent members. Initiation fees begin at $100,000. The club has 60 years of history in the community. It is managed by a Board of Directors consisting of 10 club members and the General Manager, Mr. Smith. Mr. Smith has been employed for 25 years at Fairview Country Club and is now nearing retirement age. In the past few years, Fairview has fallen on hard times and has issued yearly assessments to its membership.

Recently, during one of his weekly department head meetings, Mr. Smith discussed the current financial condition of the club. He explained that the club was in dire need of improved cash flow and that expenses had to be slashed across the board. He then handed out the previous month's profit and loss statements.

Mr. Widga, the Director of Golf, briefly examined his profit and loss statement when he returned to his office. He was surprised to see several line items, expenses, and irregularities that should not have been there. He immediately called the Controller, Ms. Nuñez, for copies of his department's profit and loss statements for the past six months. The Controller hesitated at providing the copies, but after further questioning, the paperwork was provided.

Mr. Widga carefully reviewed the reports. He soon realized that his department had not been given proper income credit. He also noted several irregular expenses that required further research and additional trips to the accounting department. The next morning, Ms. Nuñez notified Mr. Widga that she was instructed "by administration" that the club's financial statements were no longer available to employees and that information would be passed to department managers as deemed appropriate by the Board of Directors.

Concerned, Mr. Widga approached Mr. Patrick, the board member responsible for the golf department. After a long conversation about the situation, Mr. Patrick assured Mr. Widga that the situation would be resolved at the level of the Board of Directors. Mr. Patrick concluded his discussion with Mr. Widga by saying, "You were hired to run a program, not to analyze the club's financial statements." Both parties left with a clear understanding that Mr. Patrick was going to correct all of the irregularities.

In the following months, Mr. Widga began to feel that Mr. Smith was not happy with him. Knowing that his department was doing well financially, Mr. Widga tried several times to bring this to the attention of Mr. Smith. On one particular occasion Mr. Smith responded in a shocking manner, leaving Mr. Widga with an unforgettable impression. Mr. Smith had said, "Not good! How is this club supposed to survive if your department is off budget?"

This left Mr. Widga extremely confused. His records showed a year-to-date increase in net revenues, up $66,000 from the previous year. Mr. Widga again approached Mr. Patrick and the two of them went over profit and loss statements in a private meeting the following weekend. As the statements were still for the Board of Directors only, Mr. Patrick insisted that this meeting be kept between the two of them.

The following week, the president of the club asked Mr. Widga to come to the general manager's office for a brief meeting before the monthly board meeting. As the door closed, Mr. Widga was surprised to find Mr. Smith sitting at his desk. Mr. Widga had been under the impression that the meeting was between the club president and himself.

The club president and Mr. Smith made it quite clear to Mr. Widga that if he wanted to keep his job, he would refrain from speaking about his budget's irregularities immediately. In addition, he was to quit his research into the club's financial status.

Case Questions

1. Why would Mr. Smith and Mr. Patrick insist on keeping their meetings secret with Mr. Widga?

2. Two weeks later, Mr. Widga discovered that purchases from other departments had been attributed to his department and that revenue that his department generated had also been attributed to other departments. He knew the exact whereabouts of all of the money and reported it to Mr. Patrick. The next day he was fired for not following instructions. What are the issues to be considered?

3. If you were Mr. Widga, would you have done anything different? Why or why not?

4. What was Mr. Widga's main responsibility in this case?

This case was authored by Eric Johnson, Adjunct Lecturer at Johnson & Wales University, Florida Campus.

Case Study—The Ride to Paradise

West Coast Cruise Lines advertises for cruise business throughout the United States. On any given day of the week, cruise goers line up at Seattle-Tacoma International Airport, awaiting their "cruise escort" who assists them in beginning their journey to the paradise of their choice on one of West Coast's famous cruise ships.

The passengers are instructed to await their cruise escort at a predetermined location. On this particular day, Charles and Hilda Erskind arrive from Butte,

Montana. Without delay, they seek out Lawrence Gonneff, the company employee who they have been corresponding with frequently regarding their cruise. When they find him, their first question is, "How do we get to the ship? We are so excited we just can't wait to get there!"

Mr. Gonneff has tickets to the West Coast Paradise Van to sell to the Erskinds. The tickets cost $22 each. He tells them that the van is waiting right outside the luggage area of the airport. What Mr. Gonneff does not tell the Erskinds is that if they were to take a taxi to the cruise port it would only cost $25 (including tip) for a total of $12.50 per person. Mr. Gonneff does not get a commission on taxi service; he only gets commission on the tickets he sells to the West Coast Paradise Van. He rationalizes his decision not to tell the Erskinds, or any of the other passengers, about the taxi service. He assumes that if they can afford a cruise they can certainly afford the extra $19. Furthermore, the West Coast Paradise Van knows exactly where to go; a taxi driver might not. He has even heard horror stories of people being driven to the wrong port. So, he is really doing it for their benefit as well as his own. Besides, any of the passengers could have searched on the Internet for airport to cruise port transportation. If they didn't bother to do their research, why should he assist them now? He may as well make a few bucks, right?

Case Questions

1. Is Mr. Gonneff conforming to competitive business practices or is he "ripping off" the cruise passengers?

2. Has Mr. Gonneff made a sound business decision? Why or why not?

3. Would any of the ethical theories support his decision? If so, which ones? Explain your answer.

4. Would it change your evaluation if Mr. Gonneff told customers there was no other way to get to the port? Why or why not?

Case Study—The Head Shipper

Ricky Galway is the head shipper for Gourmet Victuals and Delights, Inc., commonly known as GV&D. The company has been in business since 1952 and has an excellent reputation not only for creative gift baskets but for excellent service as well. The company ships baskets, not only to the entire United States, but also to the Caribbean.

On average, Ricky gets visits from ten to fifteen salespeople per week. They represent companies such as Harry's Hungries, Lady Chocolatier, Friendly Fruits, Cook's Coffees, and more. Each of the salespeople realizes that Ricky does not decide what goes into a Gourmet Victuals and Delights gift basket. However, they respect his value to the company and, as such, they like to acknowledge his importance during the Christmas season. Each year, starting the Monday after Thanksgiving and continuing until early January, Ricky is showered with gifts from salespeople. The gifts usually are bottles of wine or liquor; occasionally he has received fine leather luggage or a gift certificate to a local high-end restaurant.

Last year, Ricky noticed that the gifts were becoming a bit pricier and it made him uncomfortable. When the saleswoman from The Heavenly Nut Company handed him two tickets to Aruba, he knew he had to do something. He spent the day pondering his dilemma.

That night, Ricky discussed his dilemma with a college instructor, Mr. Penn. After a few minutes, Mr. Penn gave Ricky an article to read by Vincent Barry. In the article Mr. Barry suggested that the following factors should be considered when evaluating the morality of accepting a gift:[11]

- What is the value of the gift? Will it influence one's decisions?
- What is the purpose of the gift? Is it, in fact, a subtle (or not so subtle) bribe?
- Why was the gift offered? Was the gift given openly? Was it given to celebrate a special event (Christmas, a birthday)?
- What is the position of the recipient of the gift? Is the recipient able to influence his own firm's dealing with the giver of the gift?
- What is accepted business practice in the industry? Is the gift typical of open and recognized industry practice?
- What is the company's policy? Does the company allow employees to accept gifts?
- What is the law? Does the law prohibit gifts of this type or for this purpose?

Case Questions

1. According to factors suggested in Mr. Barry's article, has Ricky acted in an ethical manner by accepting the gifts that he already has accepted? Explain your answer.

2. If you were in Ricky's shoes, which of the gifts, if any, would you accept? Explain your answer.

3. Why did Ricky decide to seek advice about the gifts now, when he had been accepting gifts for many years? Explain the difference between the gifts.

4. Would any of the philosophers that we have studied tell Ricky to accept the gifts? Explain your answer.

Case Study—Theresa the Telemarketer

Theresa Grady works for the Blissful Beat Telemarketing Company. Blissful Beat specializes in selling vacation packages by phone. Most potential buyers appear on Blissful Beat's call list because they signed up in shopping malls across the country for the opportunity to "win" a free cruise. Since they "willingly" offered their

---

[11] Vincent E. Barry, *Moral Issues in Business*, (Belmont, Calif.: Wadsworth, 1986), pp 237–238.

name, address, and phone number to Ready Resorts, Inc., who owns Blissful Beat, they are legally on the list even if they signed up for the national "do not call" list.

Theresa received two 6-hour days of telemarketing training (for which she was not paid). Blissful Beat explained that it was the "opportunity cost" for being hired and for being allowed to earn the high commissions that they offer for the sale of each vacation package. In training, Theresa was offered the following advice:[12]

1. Be as friendly as your "target" allows.

2. After friendliness is established, challenge the target's ego. Encourage the target to impress you, but make it difficult. For example, ask the target if he or she is a risk-taker and, if they say yes, encourage them to provide illustrations.

3. After gently putting down one or two of the illustrations, ask if the target trusts you. Encourage back and forth discussion until you can get a "yes" or as close as you can come to a "yes" regarding trust.

4. The next lines could look something like this:

   "Why don't you want to purchase this vacation? Either you trust me or you don't and I'm telling you it's a great deal. I'll also let you in on a secret. If folks don't buy this package, it is for only one of two reasons—either because they don't trust me or they can't afford it. Which one is it?"

5. The next very important step is to get the target to take out his or her credit card. A few questions that usually help are: "Does your middle initial appear on your credit card? What is the date of expiration on your credit card? Does your credit card have a gold seal on the front?" Use whatever you think will work with your target. You will be the expert at that point.

6. And, *voilà*—you have sealed the deal. At this point, you can count on pocketing your commission!

Theresa, a single mother, was thrilled to find this job. It is close to home and she can work the hours she wants. She was also told that she might be able to work at home in the evening after she becomes established with the company.

However, after two weeks Theresa is becoming increasingly uncomfortable. She feels like she is fooling people because she knows that the "vacation" is really one big advertisement for Ready Resorts, Inc. During the "vacation" the guests are continually bombarded with information about Ready Resorts timeshares. The first night they are offered a free steak dinner (wine included). But they are not told that during the dinner there is a presentation.

Theresa would like to resign from her job but has not even been paid to date. After working for one week, she had made a grand total of $150 and, of that

---

[12] Ideas for this exchange were taken from an article in *The New Times*, January 8–14, 2004, pp. 7–10.

money, she will not see $75 for another three months because the company has a policy that places a hold on your first three sales.

Case Questions

1. In your opinion, did Blissful Beat have the right to conceal the fact that they would try to sell their customers timeshares with Ready Resorts?

2. Look over the five preparation suggestions that Theresa received in her training class. Explain each suggestion individually according to the different philosophical theories we have studied: utilitarianism, categorical imperative, justice, and virtue.

3. Does the company have the right to hold Theresa's wages? If it is legal, is it also ethical? Why or why not?

4. What would you do if you were in Theresa's shoes?

7

Applying Ethics to the Maintenance and Housekeeping Functions

THE UPKEEP OF A PROPERTY is a major responsibility. Safety, security, and cleanliness are of paramount importance to any visitor who stays in a hotel or who eats at a food service establishment. Whether guests are businessmen, families with small children, single women, or elderly couples—everyone wants to feel secure in a clean and comfortable environment. They want to enjoy the amenities promised.

From a well-lit walkway to a hallway night-light to sparkling restrooms, maintenance and housekeeping employees must consider the guest and work accordingly. These behind-the-scene tasks come to the forefront only when there is a problem. The smoother these back-of-the-house activities function, the more comfortable guests are and this translates into a good business reputation and repeat visitors.

Problems occur when matters other than the safety, security, and comfort of the guest overshadow the necessary work of maintaining a property. Maintenance and housekeeping must work in concert to properly maintain a property. That is why maintenance and housekeeping are often kept under one umbrella in hospitality organizations.

The safety of the employees is an important matter as well. In 1970, the Occupational Safety and Health Administration (OSHA) was created to protect workers from hazards in the workplace and to also ensure that they be informed of hazards at the workplace.[1] In housekeeping this could refer to the use of dangerous chemicals; in maintenance it could refer to working with hazardous machinery.

The case below, "On the Edge," is followed by detailed ethical analyses in relation to each of the ethical theories presented earlier: utilitarianism, Kant's categorical imperative, Rawls's justice ethics, and Aristotle's ethics of virtue. The chapter closes with a series of case studies and questions about the cases that challenge you to analyze ethical issues in areas of maintenance and housekeeping.

---

[1] Linda K. Treviño and Katherine A. Nelson, *Managing Business Ethics: Straight Talk About How to Do It Right*, 3d ed. (Hoboken, N.J.: Wiley, 2004), p. 208.

Case Study—On the Edge

The Edgewater Hotel Group is so-named because it selects hotel sites that are nearby or adjacent to large bodies of water. It is a substantial hotel group with 110 properties worldwide; 95 properties are in the United States, the rest are located in Western Europe. Because they are such a sizeable hotel concern they have always received an excellent liability insurance rate. Their insurance company was recently sold to Commensality, Inc., one of the largest insurance companies in the world. The new owners have been reviewing all insurance rates and have decided that The Edgewater Hotel Group is underpaying for their liability insurance because there have been several deaths, severe injuries, and large claim payouts over the last five years. All disbursements have been related to the swimming and boating areas.

Marcus Birch, President and CEO of the Edgewater Hotel Group, received a letter from Commensality, Inc., stating that their insurance liability rates would be rising, on average, $5,000 per property per year ($550,000 a year) unless the hotel concern updated and modernized many of its safety features. Commensality Inc. included statistics and research reports showing how each new safety measure would improve the overall safety standards for the Edgewater Hotel Group. Birch was rather surprised as he read from the report that the inclusion of one or more of the following would bring great savings on Edgewater's liability insurance rates. As he read, he also realized that each improvement came at a cost to the Edgewater Hotel Group. The excerpt that he chose to highlight for his Maintenance Chief, Mr. Richard Brick, follows:

1. *Higher life-guard stands*

   a. *Allows for greater visibility on large bodies of water*

   b. *Cost = $300 per lifeguard stand located on large body of water*

   c. *Shown to decrease death and serious injuries by 80%;*

   Shown to decrease claim expenditures by 18%

2. *Test water for E. coli and other microorganisms on a daily basis*

   a. *Microorganism contamination of swimming waters causes foodborne illness outbreaks (swallowing contaminated waters)*

   b. *Cost includes testing of each body of water everyday; average cost estimated at $12/day per property*

   c. *Shown to decrease death and illness by 65%;*

Shown to decrease claim expenditures by 10%

3. *Erect a barrier to swimming near coastal bluffs*

   a. *Coastal bluffs are a dangerous natural hazard found along any coastline; estimated annual deaths total approximately 80 per year*

   b. *Estimated cost involves costs associated with building a fence able to keep swimmers out of dangerous areas; average cost estimated at $2,000 per property*

   c. *Shown to decrease death and serious injuries by 88%;*

   Shown to decrease claim expenditures by 32%

After much deliberation about the letter from Commensality, Inc., Mr. Birch called in his Maintenance Chief, Mr. Richard Brick. Birch gave Brick a copy of the letter, highlighting the above excerpt. He also included the following assignment in writing:

"Send out bids for the three suggested safety improvements noted above. Based on the lowest bid that comes in, check with accounting to see if it will be worth our while to make the recommended improvements. Inform accounting that it is necessary to include all "breakeven" points. For example, it is estimated that Property #26 will expend $400,000 in injury and death claims over the next five years. If the suggested improvements are made to Property #26, will it cost more or less than $400,000? I would like this information on my desk three weeks from today."

What appears to be Mr. Birch's main concern? Is the consideration of a breakeven point an ethical matter when the safety of guests is concerned? An article appeared in *The New York Times* on January 29, 1995, entitled, "How Much for a Life? Try $3 Million to $5 Million."[2] The article quotes Kip Viscusi, an economist at Duke University, who estimated that if the entire gross national product were devoted to making life safe, there would only be $55 million available to prevent each accidental death.[3] Does that mean that we should spend money on safety only as long as there is enough left over for everything else we want to do? Should we test water for *E. coli* and other microorganisms on a daily basis or reupholster the lobby furniture? If the cost to the company is exactly the same for each item, but there is only enough money for a single expenditure, does the question become which will bring in more guests and, therefore, more income?

When thinking about safety and security, a hospitality entity has a responsibility to the guest. However, it also has a responsibility to its shareholders. In many instances the decision will become *is it worth the cost to the company?*

---

[2] Peter Passell, "How Much for a Life? Try $3 Million to $5 Million," *The New York Times,* January 29, 1995, sec. 3, p. 3.

[3] *Ibid.*

🔍 Case Commentary: Utilitarianism

A utilitarian would approach this dilemma by identifying the alternative actions and their consequences for all stakeholders. For example, if expenditures for improvements at property #37 will be $800,000 but savings in insurance payments are estimated to be only $400,000, then Edgewater should not do the improvements. This is an example of comparing the harms to the benefits for the company. The utilitarian approach can be extremely practical when thinking through this type of ethical dilemma. But it can also be unwieldy to calculate the harms and benefits to each and every Edgewater property and base the decision for that particular property solely on the calculations.

In addition, we have to consider if, when using this strictly consequentialist method, we are really evaluating all of the consequences for all of the stakeholders. For example, are we thinking about the pain and grief that will unquestionably occur if even one fatality were to take place? Have we taken into consideration all of the stakeholders that would be affected in that regard: all of the family, friends, co-workers, neighbors, etc., of the deceased?

A utilitarian might also look at this problem from the view of maximizing societal welfare. In this case, the decision would still involve money because if the dollars were not used for safety and security, they might be used for other improvements that could also benefit society. For example, if the hotel does not purchase the higher lifeguard stands, management would have the money to hire three new front desk agents. This would not only ease the check-in check-out lines, but would bring three new jobs, with benefits, to the community. This approach would still involve costing out the benefits and the harms to the society and choosing the approach that would bring the most benefit.

Another way utilitarianism would look at maximizing social welfare would be by calculating the total harms to all of society from the accidents and deaths if improvements are not made. While the insurance costs of an accidental injury may be "X" dollars, the total costs to all of society (ongoing medical costs, lost contribution from a formerly productive worker, etc.) might be 4 or 5 times "X" dollars. This could change the balance decisively regarding whether the expenditure for an improvement was worthwhile. However, it would probably also change the calculation for who should be paying for which share of the total cost, since we are now calculating costs and benefits to the entire society, not simply to the Edgewater Hotel Group. Consequently, maybe society as a whole (through government expenditures, for example) should pick up some of the costs for an improvement proportionate to its share of lowered costs if the improvements were made.

🔍 Case Commentary: Kant's Categorical Imperative

Kant would offer a different view of potential solutions. A deontologist would certainly say it is one's duty to protect his fellow man. More specifically, the officials of the Edgewater administration would search their consciences asking, "What is my duty now that I know of the potential harm to my guests?" A Kantian thinker's decision would be based on the formulation of broad, universal principles that relate specifically to the Edgewater dilemma such as the right to safety and security, compassion for all humanity, respect for the sanctity of life, and so on.

Deontological thinkers often use reasoning very close to the golden rule, which says to treat others the way you would like to be treated. The golden rule would ask, if Marcus Birch were to go to a hotel with his wife and children, wouldn't he want the safety of his family members assured? How much would he pay for what amount of safety? Whatever that amount is, he should provide the same degree of safety at all Edgewater properties.

But the Kantian perspective is slightly different. The golden rule still relies on consequences of actions as the basis for ethical decisions, and as such it is still a variation of, or closely related to, utilitarianism. Kant would tell us to ignore the consequences when making a moral judgment, but to instead pay attention to the principle or rule being followed if you adopt one course of action or another. Could you make the principle into a universal rule? The universal rule, "Do whatever is cost-effective regarding safety measures," is not obviously self-contradictory, so simply following a utilitarian cost-benefit analysis of safety issues may pass the test posed by the first formulation of Kant's categorical imperative (be able to make the principle of your action into a universal rule).

However, the second formulation of the categorical imperative poses the question a little more sharply: are you turning another human being into a mere means (degrading him or her from being a person into a mere "thing"), rather than treating human beings as ends-in-themselves? Are you risking a death or a serious injury simply for the sake of a profit margin? On the other hand, you cannot make a property absolutely safe in all respects. So, Mr. Birch will have to decide at which point is he denying "personhood" to other persons if he chooses not to institute safety measures because of financial consideration. Going past that point is immoral, according to Kant.

Deciding when you are crossing the boundary and treating other human beings merely as means to your own goals (i.e., turning them into "things") is not always easy. Perhaps a good rule to follow is to apply that old stand-by, the golden rule. If you would not want others to do it to you, you are probably acting unethically by degrading others to the status of a "thing" (a means, not an end). That is why the golden rule is so closely related to Kantian ethics. If Mr. Birch is to act morally according to Kantian ethics, he will need to institute all safety measures he would want for himself if he were a guest. This may require more expenditure than a utilitarian cost-benefit analysis would justify. Kantian ethics may be stricter than utilitarian ethics in cases such as this.

⌕ Case Commentary: The Ethic of Justice

How would an ethic of justice apply to this case? Clearly, if guests are exposed to abnormally hazardous conditions at Edgewater properties without fair warning, an injustice will occur. This violates Rawls's principle of equal liberty: each person in an institution has an equal right to the most extensive liberty compatible with a like liberty for all. On the other hand, if Edgewater properties have safety practices that seem reasonably fair to even those most likely to be injured or killed (e.g., guests and some categories of employees), they are probably just.

Rawls would say that the decision regarding the justice or injustice of Edgewater's safety practices is best made behind the "veil of ignorance." That is, make the decision without knowing if you are going to end up as a customer, an Edgewater shareholder, Mr. Birch, a maintenance worker, a lifeguard, the concierge, etc. This way, you will probably be conscientious about safety because you may end up being the person most exposed to danger. But, at the same time, you would not push safety to absurd lengths where you end up harming most people merely for a minuscule, marginal improvement in safety outcomes.

In practice, Rawls's ethic of justice in this case would probably come to conclusions quite close to those of a Kantian. Both would be remarkably close to an application of the golden rule, because both would put primary emphasis on protection of the interests of the most vulnerable, although neither would push this to absurd lengths. But both ethical theories might be more stringent and demanding on Mr. Birch and the Edgewater Hotel Group than utilitarianism, which may require only a cost-benefit analysis.

One aspect where an ethic of justice may be particularly applicable is at the level of public policy and public regulation. For example, which regulations should be in place to *require* Edgewater and similar institutions to provide a safe environment for its guests and its employees? Rather than leaving it up to the individual businesses, society may wish to require all enterprises in a particular line of business to abide by certain regulations. For example, warning signs may be required. Lifeguards in some places during certain hours may be required. In deciding what is, or is not, warranted in the form of required legal regulations, the Rawlsian *original position* behind the "veil of ignorance" may be a most useful perspective to use. Justice ethics can be easily applied in public policy discussions.

Case Commentary: Aristotle and the Ethics of Virtue

The virtue ethics approach focuses more on the integrity of the decision maker than on the ethical act itself. A virtue ethics perspective primarily considers a person's character.

Which decision would indicate a virtuous character? Several virtues are relevant here. Justice, as already noted, is one. Prudence, or wisdom, would be another. Compassion and sensitivity would be two more. Aristotle would call on Mr. Birch to practice these virtues and to make a decision in accordance with them. If Mr. Birch's decision were unjust, lacking in compassion, insensitive, or imprudent, we would judge him accordingly.

While it is impossible to set up rigid rules to follow, people of good character will have little difficulty in making a judgment. An individual's community becomes their guide. What is the accepted practice within that community? In the case of the Edgewater Hotel Chain, the community is a professional community, but one that also includes guests as well as employees.

If you, the hotel manager, were to make a decision based on virtue ethics, you could ask yourself, *"Within my community, would I be proud to bring up the decision openly?"* As a hotel manager, would I publicize the fact that I chose to purchase new furniture for the lobby instead of purchasing higher lifeguard stands that would ensure greater safety? Would I be proud to tell my decision to fellow businessmen at the next chamber of commerce meeting? Would I be proud to tell my decision to the parents at the Girl Scout meeting held on property this afternoon? Would I be proud to tell my decision to my extended family at our upcoming Thanksgiving dinner? If the answer to all or some of these questions is "No," we can assume the action, according to virtue ethics, may be morally problematic.

Consider the Edgewater Hotel Group specifically. If Mr. Birch decides not to make the safety improvements in order to use the money in some other manner, would he be willing to see that information publicized on the front page of all the local newspapers in the cities where Edgewater has properties? If he is not willing to see this information made public, then he has doubts about the virtue of his character as demonstrated by this decision.

Case Study—The VIP

It was a beautiful, sunny Florida day with blue skies, scattered clouds, and low humidity. It was a perfect day for the beach. No one could be happier than Richard Jackson, the General Manager of the Great Escapes Beach Resort. He has a full house in the hotel and he is expecting a famous celebrity to arrive today. All the preparations are in place as requested by J.J. Morony, the famous basketball player.

Richard Jackson personally went about ensuring that all the amenities, as well as the necessities, were in the suite. He was being quite particular as Mr. Morony insisted on having the Sportsman Deluxe Suite, the only one of its kind in South Florida. He was also being quite particular because he was a bit worried. The hotel sprinkler system had been acting up recently. It had unexpectedly gone off in the Sportsman Suite just two weeks ago. Thankfully, no one had been occupying it at the time. He had been assured by Deluxe Maintenance Inc. that the problem was a faulty heating switch and everything was now in perfect working order. But the hotel's Director of Maintenance, Mr. Wilder, was not convinced that the problem was just the faulty heating switch. He thought the entire system was in need of an overhaul and continually told Mr. Jackson that this was the case.

Mr. Jackson listened respectfully to Mr. Wilder. Then he explained, "We cannot give up the extra dollars that the Sportsman Suite will bring us. The revenue from that suite alone is more than four times the revenue of a normal room."

The Great Escapes Beach Resort is a four-star, 320-room hotel boasting of three restaurants and a luxurious spa. The resort has a stunning view of the Gulf Coast. For the last 25 years, the resort earned a great reputation with both its guests and the community. In recent months, the resort had undergone a number of minor renovations in the lobby and on some of the guest floors. However, the property was scheduled for major renovations towards the end of summer, which would last for several months.

During last month's executive meeting, which included all department heads, a final report was handed to Mr. Jackson, highlighting several major problems that needed to be addressed as soon as possible. Especially alarming was the report from the engineering department about the operational status of the fire sprinkler system in all the guestrooms.

Mr. Jackson assured every one present that all repairs would be taken care of at the end of the season. He also mentioned that they had several celebrities visiting over the next two months and all repairs would have to wait. He did not want to have the celebrities inconvenienced. And, he wanted their repeat business as well. Mr. Jackson also stated that he was already in receipt of the estimates necessary for the upcoming repairs to the sprinkler system, and that work would begin promptly when the season was finished. At the end of the meeting, during his summary statement, Mr. Jackson urged everyone present to all work together as one team and help each other until the renovation was completed.

Mr. Jackson was in his office when he received a call from the front office announcing the arrival of J.J. Morony. He immediately went to the lobby where he greeted his guest and his family. After a tour of the resort, Mr. Jackson escorted them to their suite. As he was leaving the room, Mr. Jackson suggested to Mr. Morony to try the beach. "This is one of the best days I've seen here in a long time. You and your family should definitely take advantage of the opportunity."

A few hours later, Richard Jackson received a call from Mr. Edwards, the beach hut manger saying that Mr. Morony and his family took his advice. "They're all on the beach and seem to be having a fine time," Edwards told Jackson.

Later that day, Mr. Jackson was having lunch with several of his business partners at a restaurant located about a mile from the resort. During the luncheon, he received a call from Mr. Plotkin, the head of the security department at the resort. Mr. Plotkin told Mr. Jackson that there was a faulty fire sprinkler on the 5th floor in the west wing where all the full Gulf view suites are located. This included the celebrity's suite. The initial report was that all of the guests' belongings were either damaged or thoroughly soaked as a result of the sprinklers.

Case Questions

1. What are the ethical issues in this case? Explain your answer.

2. Why does Mr. Jackson find himself in such an untenable situation?

3. What should Mr. Jackson have done differently?

4. How should the Great Escapes Beach Resort compensate J.J. Morony?

5. How would someone who is operating from behind "the veil of ignorance" view this situation? Explain your answer.

6. What ethical rule or rules should Mr. Jackson consider for the future?

This case was authored by Samer Hassan, Ph.D., Associate Professor of Hospitality Management at Johnson & Wales University, Florida Campus.

Case Study—The Housekeeper's Paycheck

The Bushman Resort and Spa is located an hour's drive northwest of Austin, Texas, along the Colorado River. Family owned and operated for 30 years, the resort was built on property that had been in the Bushman family since 1858. In

1970, the family sold off 1,200 acres of land, along with several buildings that belonged to the original ranch. Total selling price was $14.2 million.

The cost of building the resort was approximately $6 million. Most costs were financed by a local savings and loan association owned by Mr. Jibber Chaney, a Bushman cousin on the maternal side of the family. William Bushman, the present CEO and owner of the Bushman Resort, is the great, great, great grandson of the original William Bushman who settled the property after giving up his journey to California to find gold in 1856.

The resort boasts of 185 all-suite guestrooms on 450 acres of wilderness that winds its way along the Colorado River. The site offers guests total privacy. Prices are high, ranging from $300 to $1,200 per night, excluding the executive guest suites. These run $2,000 to $4,000 per night.

Offerings at the Bushman Resort include a full service spa and health club, fourteen tennis courts, horseback riding, two executive 18-hole golf courses, river rafting and other river activities, and four heated swimming pools (two outdoor, two indoor). There is also an onsite dinner theater and a movie theater as well as seven restaurants, three of which are open twenty-four hours, seven days per week. In order to maintain the very high level of service that the clients have come to expect, there is a 1:1 ratio of guests to employees. At all times, there are as many employees on staff as there are guests.

Occupancy rates over the last two years have varied greatly, especially in summer. Whereas the 1980s saw summer occupancy rates ranging from 85% to 95%, summer occupancy rates have lately declined to 65%. In his office conservatory overlooking the main garden, Mr. Bushman examined the latest occupancy statistics. He was quite distressed about the most recent summer occupancy percentages and called in his General Manager, Ms. Candy Leman, to discuss improvements.

"Our biggest cost is labor as you well know Candy," Mr. Bushman explained. "We are going to have to find some way to reduce our labor cost and yet maintain our high level of service. If we don't maintain our high service levels, we won't attract the right type of clientele."

Ms. Leman took the papers from Mr. Bushman and looked them over.

"How much do we pay our housekeepers?" Mr. Bushman inquired when she finished reading the report.

"$10 per hour." Candy responded.

Bushman was aghast. "Why, that's criminal! Why are we paying them so much above the minimum wage?"

"Because if they are paid well, they do a better job." Candy replied.

"Do they all have proper documentation? You know, green cards, citizenship, etc?" He then lowered his voice and continued in a conspiratorial manner, "Do we have any undocumented workers that are earning money off the books?"

"No, not that I know of," Candy answered.

"Well there's your answer then. We'll save lots of money that way. Start laying off the higher paid housekeepers and look for employees who don't have proper papers. They'll work for next to nothing. Also, we can lay them off and rehire them as we see fit and they won't complain. So, if one week our occupancy is down, we'll just tell a few of them not to come in."

Candy was very quiet, so Bushman continued. "How many rooms does each housekeeper do per day? Eight?"

Candy nodded that he was correct.

"Well, those new workers will just have to work a bit more quickly. They'll each do 10. Or maybe even 12."

It was Candy's turn to look aghast. "I can't do that Mr. Bushman. I know these people. They do a good job. Some of them have worked for us for more than 10 years."

Bushman thought it over silently for a few minutes. "You'll do it, or you'll be the first one to leave," he stated.

Case Questions

1. In your judgment, are Mr. Bushman's suggestions ethical? Why or why not?

2. If you were in Ms. Leman's shoes, what would you do? Explain your answer.

3. How would a utilitarian look at Mr. Bushman's suggestions?

4. Apply Rawls's ethic of justice to this case.

Case Study—Dissatisfaction

The Chalworth Hotel is located on 50 acres of prime property in eastern suburban Long Island. The main building is registered as an historic landmark. The hotel was built in 1935 when the area was mostly farmland and it has continued to expand, slowly but surely, for almost 75 years. In fact, the local historical society is planning a birthday celebration for the hotel in the year 2010. Plans are already underway.

The owners of the original Chalworth Hotel were Margaret and John Chalworth of London, England. They were uncomfortable with the politics in Europe at the time and brought over their very large family: 4 sons, 2 daughters, along with both his and her parents. The hotel, worked mostly by family members, had become well known not only for its excellent European service, but for afternoon tea as well. Family members owned the hotel until 1998, when the last remaining Chalworth decided to sell to the international hotel corporation, the S-Group. The hotel has been owned and managed by the S-Group since the 1998 purchase.

At the time of sale, occupancy was at an all-time low; the average annual occupancy rate for the previous 5 years had been 55%. However, from 1945 to 1975, occupancy averaged close to 90% per year.

Originally a 12-room hotel, The Chalworth now has 72 guestrooms in 3 buildings, a heated indoor-outdoor swimming pool, 2 lighted tennis courts, and many private park-like seating areas around the grounds.

This past September, the Graff family decided to revisit the hotel. Bernie and Betty Graff had honeymooned there in September 1965 and were now celebrating their 40th anniversary. They noted quite a few changes, many of them to their dissatisfaction. Bernie decided to write the following note to Mr. Rogers, the present General Manager of the Chalworth Hotel:

Dear Mr. Rogers:

I have been a guest at the Chalworth Hotel many times over the past 40 years. I have never been as disappointed as I was with this last visit. I will detail for you some of the reasons for my dissatisfaction.

I was unable to swim because the "heated" water in the swimming pool was very cold (no more than 75 degrees F.). The air in the indoor pool area was too cold as well; my wife and I were even too uncomfortable to sit in that pool area without wearing a sweater.

There was a cracked window in our guestroom. The paint on the walls was peeling. The gardens were overgrown. The benches were chipped. And where were all the bird feeders?

On our first evening at the Chalworth, my wife and I went out to play tennis but the lights were not on. When we inquired at the front desk, we were told that the courts were only lit during July and August. It was a lovely September evening and we were quite disappointed.

I am writing to you because I want to enjoy future visits at the Chalworth Hotel. I fear, now that the hotel is no longer family-owned, the place will become non-descript. I am also writing because your most recent advertisement in the Sunday New York Times states: "heated pool, lighted tennis courts, beautifully manicured grounds, refurbished rooms—all in an atmosphere our guests have come to expect over the years." It is my opinion that you must deliver what you claim or not advertise like this any longer.

Sincerely, Bernie Graff

Mr. Rogers mulled over the note from Mr. Graff. He decided to call in his Director of Maintenance, Arnold Spencer. When Mr. Spencer arrived, Mr. Rogers handed him the note. Spencer read it through carefully. When he was finished he looked up and waited expectantly.

"Well?" Mr. Rogers inquired. "What have you to say for yourself?"

"You put us on a very tight budget three months ago. You cut our electricity budget in half. You 'trimmed'—your words—my workforce. Every time I have come to you with a maintenance budget request you have turned me down. You wouldn't even allow us to replace the very old, very broken riding mower. How do you expect 50 acres of grounds to be kept manicured without a decent mower? You told me to make do with what I have. And that is what I have been doing—to the best of my ability."

Case Questions

1. What are the ethical issues in this case? Explain your answer.

2. In their approaches to this case, how would a rule utilitarian differ from an act utilitarian? Explain your answer.

3. How would a justice ethicist resolve this case?

4. If you were in command of this hotel, what would you do? Why?

Case Study—Only Your Housekeeper Knows for Sure

Ms. Leslie Hunter had been a housekeeper for the Brightman Spa Resort for eight years. She had worked her way into housekeeping management two years ago and was quite proud of the fact. She had built an excellent staff. Morale was high; absentee and turnover rates were low.

Three months ago, Mr. Antonio Mitchell became the Assistant Manager for the resort. He was young and ambitious, and Ms. Hunter did not trust him. She knew that he cut corners and he had tried to pressure her to add additional duties to the housekeepers' workdays without additional pay. To date, she had refused.

This morning, Mr. Mitchell brought Ms. Hunter two cases of gallon jars of generic shampoo. He also brought her several thousand empty, recycled, individual-sized shampoo bottles. The labels on the bottles were *Haute Hair*, a well-known, very exclusive salon product that the hotel had been using for the past several years. Mr. Mitchell's instructions were simple: fill the *Haute Hair* bottles with generic shampoo. Assign each housekeeper 200 bottles to fill each shift until the job is finished.

Ms. Hunter was flabbergasted. She was in a total quandary. She was unwilling to do the job herself, and she was also unwilling to assign it to anyone else. To make matters worse, she had only recently found out that Mr. Mitchell was the son of one of the hotel owner's best friends.

Case Questions

1. List the benefits and harms done if Ms. Hunter follows Mr. Mitchell's instructions. Also, state who benefits and who is harmed.

2. From a utilitarian perspective, is there anything wrong with what Mr. Mitchell is requesting? Explain your answer.

3. What would Kant say about this situation? Explain your answer.

4. What would you do if you were Ms. Hunter? Explain your answer.

Case Study—The Renovation

John Owens is the owner and General Manger of the Beach View Hotel. This contemporary, 300-room hotel was built in the late 1980s and overlooks a white sandy beach. In recent years, the hotel has built an excellent reputation with its guests. The Beach View Hotel enjoys 80% occupancy year round. The best time for business is during summer when occupancy reaches 100%.

For the last few years, Mr. Owens had been considering a major renovation to the property, but he continually postponed the project for different reasons. Last week, while he was in a meeting with his executive team discussing final preparations for the summer season, the Housekeeping Director, Mrs. Smithson, told him that a number of rooms on the fifth floor were flooded because of a roof leak. Mrs.

Smithson reminded Mr. Owens that during previous meetings she had told him of the stifling smell in some of the rooms on the fifth floor and that guests also had complained several times. The Director of Engineering, Mr. Landsman, spoke up immediately. He stated that according to previous roof inspections, the recommendation was that the hotel needed a new roof.

Mr. Owens acknowledged that he had been told about the roof in earlier meetings but he wanted to wait until after the busy summer season so as not to disturb his guests. He further stated that replacing the roof would not be an easy task, and that the workers and equipment in the hotel would definitely disturb the guests. However, shortly after the meeting, Mr. Owens did start calling a number of roofing companies to get estimates. The prices varied greatly, but each company agreed that it would take approximately 6-8 weeks to get the job done.

The hotel's advertisements all stated *"a peaceful, quiet location on the beach."* Mr. Owens thought about the summer season and the many guests that would be visiting the Beach View Hotel: "What will I tell the guests when they arrive? Should I inform the guests who have existing reservations? When new guests call for reservations, should I mention the construction? Maybe I should just cancel the summer season?"

Mr. Owens thought about his dilemma for a few days. Finally, he decided not to mention anything to either the already existing reservations or to potential guests when they called for summer reservations. He would give each guest a note upon arrival, stating that the hotel was undergoing emergency repairs and that he was very sorry for the inconvenience. He would also offer $100 dining credit in the hotel's restaurant.

Case Questions

1. Is Mr. Owens acting in an ethical manner? Explain your answer.

2. How would you handle the situation that Mr. Owens is facing? Explain your answer.

This case was authored by Samer Hassan, Ph.D., Associate Professor of Hospitality Management at Johnson & Wales University, Florida Campus.

8

Applying Ethics to the Food and Beverage Function

WHENEVER GUESTS enter a restaurant they have the right to be served safe food prepared under sanitary conditions. When discussing the ethics involved in a food service operation, matters such as these are central. Sanitation concerns such as "use-by" dates are one example. Is it permissible to take the attitude, "Oh, that's only two days past the 'use-by' date—it's perfectly okay!"? Other examples of irresponsible behavior are serving food held at inappropriate temperatures and allowing unsanitary conditions in kitchen areas. Ethical issues can quickly become complicated by the pressures of daily operations. What would you do if your supervisor orders you to serve food that you know has been kept in the temperature danger zone for more than four hours?

Just as serious are cases involving outright cheating of guests. Guests have the right to receive what they order. This involves not only the ingredients of items described on the menu but advertised portion sizes as well. Salespeople are known to exaggerate the qualities of their products. But, is it acceptable for a restaurateur to exaggerate so much that guests think they are eating fresh fish when, in fact, the fish has been frozen? Or, is it acceptable to lead guests to believe that they are eating an organic product when it is not? When skirting the truth about a product is more than just hype, it is unethical. Similar to product safety, truth in advertising, which includes truth in menu, is an issue for both organizations and individuals.[1] Truth in menu is an ethical issue because it involves fairness, honesty, and respect for others.

There are plenty of opportunities for cheating, stealing, and other wrongful behaviors within a food and beverage operation. However, guests have the right to expect safe food when they dine out. Additionally, it is a basic consumer right to be told the truth concerning the products and services purchased. This includes full disclosure regarding food and beverage products. One of the fastest ways to lose customers is to be dishonest with them.

The case below, "A Good Job Pays Your Bills," is followed by ethical analyses in relation to utilitarianism, Kant's categorical imperative, Rawls's justice ethics, and Aristotle's ethics of virtue. The chapter closes with a series of case studies and

---

[1] Linda K. Treviño and Katherine A. Nelson, *Managing Business Ethics: Straight Talk About How to Do It Right*, 3d ed. (Hoboken, N.J.: Wiley, 2004), p. 72.

questions about the cases that challenge you to analyze ethical issues that arise in food and beverage operations.

Case Study—A Good Job Pays Your Bills

> *Mr. Mason is the food and beverage manager of the 550-room Gem Hotel in the Catskill Mountains of New York. As part of his job, every three months, he prepares a "forecasted income statement" for the hotel's food and beverage department.*
>
> *This past September, when preparing the statement, he was costing out the menu for the winter season and realized that the price of meat products had gone up by 8% to 12%. He questioned the purveyor, Best Deal Food, Inc. The purveyor's reason for the price hike was the heavy snow en route to the Catskills from New York. He clarified further by explaining that the delivery trucks that brought the products from New York were also charging higher prices.*
>
> *Mr. Mason brought his findings to Mr. Maxwell, the owner of the hotel. Mr. Maxwell looked Mr. Mason straight in the eye and said, "Fix it, that's your job. The bottom line pays your good salary and bonus."*
>
> *In as measured a tone as he could muster, Mr. Mason replied, "I will have to print new menus with a price increase." Mr. Maxwell stared at him in disbelief, put his arm around Mr. Mason's shoulder and said, "Printing new leather-bound menus is expensive, and many of our regular customers will be offended with a price increase. You are a food man—just reduce the portion size, but leave on the old price. Give them a great plate presentation!"*
>
> *Mr. Mason immediately realized that Mr. Maxwell wanted him to short change customers by camouflaging the main entrée with starches and vegetables so they would never know it was a 10 oz. steak instead of the 12 oz. steak mentioned on the menu. He would have to do the same thing with all of the meat, chicken, and fish products.*

This case was authored by Jude Ferreira, Assistant Professor of Hospitality Management, Johnson & Wales University, Florida Campus.

Federal and state laws apply to this case. Both the federal law and the law of virtually every state include statutes that prohibit the use of deceptive or unfair trade practices. The Federal Trade Commission (FTC), the principal federal agency protecting consumer interests, enforces the law. Under this federal law, the capacity to deceive, and not actual deception, is prohibited. Therefore, the FTC is not required to prove that deception actually occurred. If an advertisement, statement, or brochure fails to disclose important information there may be a violation.

In addition, most states have now adopted either the Uniform Deceptive Trade Practices Act or their own similar laws. These laws protect consumers and other businesses. The Uniform Deceptive Trade Practices Act provides that a person or business has engaged in an illegal deceptive trade practice when (in addition to many other things) goods or services are represented as of a particular standard, quality or grade, or of a particular style or model, when they are not.

Clearly, there are legal dimensions that apply to many ethical situations. However, "legal" decisions or outcomes are not necessarily "ethical" decisions or outcomes. If prosecuted for deceptive business practices, Mr. Mason and Mr. Maxwell would hire attorneys who would defend them in relation to the rules of law. The following sections view the situation of Mr. Mason and Mr. Maxwell from strictly ethical points of view and seek to judge them not in the legal terms of guilt or innocence—but in moral terms of right or wrong.

Case Commentary: Utilitarianism

Utilitarianism looks at the consequences of our actions. There will be consequences for all of the stakeholders involved if Mr. Mason follows Mr. Maxwell's orders to decrease portion sizes and deceive guests into thinking they are getting the same amount of food promised by the menu. Who exactly are the stakeholders? They are Mr. Maxwell, Mr. Mason, all of the kitchen employees who would be involved in the deception and, of course, the guests.

Mr. Maxwell is cheating many people in order to enrich himself. The losses of the many outweigh the gains to a few, and because of this, act utilitarians would say he is behaving in an unethical manner. Additionally, rule utilitarians would say that the deception is morally unacceptable because rules of conduct allowing such deceptive behaviors will lead to more harm than good. A rule utilitarian would ask, "What would be the consequences if all restaurants lied about portion sizes on their menus?" Or, "What would be the consequences if everyone cheated in their business dealings?"

Mr. Maxwell is breaking a moral rule of society (to tell the truth) if he lies on his menu. What about Mr. Mason? He is only following orders. If he does not follow orders, he will lose his job. Is it acceptable for Mr. Mason to cheat the guests? Mr. Mason needs to ask himself which moral rules he is willing to live by. A rule utilitarian would suggest to Mr. Mason that, in this case, the rule he should follow is the rule that says we all should treat each other fairly and honestly.

Of course, this case is not just a simple matter. Suppose Mr. Mason is the sole support of his family? Suppose jobs are very scarce? Suppose he has a huge mortgage and other monthly payments to make? However, at the end of the day, he has to live with his own actions. Is he willing to expose himself as a con artist to all of the kitchen employees? If he did, he would also be telling them that it is acceptable to defraud guests.

Case Commentary: Kant's Categorical Imperative

Kant would examine the behaviors of both Mr. Maxwell and Mr. Mason. Remember, Kant judges a person based on the reason for their actions. Kant would find Mr. Maxwell's actions unethical because cheating of this nature violates the *categorical imperative* to always treat other human beings as ends, not merely as means for your own purposes. Do you think Kant would be just as quick to condemn Mr.

Mason whose job might be at stake? You might think he would be more lenient because Mr. Mason has so much to lose, but remember that Kant's *categorical imperative* states that there are rules that we always must follow—not only when it is convenient.

Therefore, Mr. Mason should not cheat because he could not make it a universal rule that everyone can cheat. If Mr. Mason attempted to universalize his decision, he would have to ask himself if his choice to deceive the guests by camouflaging the entrées would be a suitable decision for all of the other managers and employees of the hotel. According to Kant, if Mr. Mason thought that his decision was appropriate and that he was treating others as humans (ends) rather than as things (means), then it would be suitable to broadcast it to the other managers and employees of the hotel. In other words, it would be acceptable for all managers and employees to deceive the hotel guests. Front desk clerks could sell deluxe rooms, but place guests in regular rooms. Bellmen could carry guests' luggage to their rooms, and then falsely state that there is a charge. Servers could add tips to customers' credit card charges, and so forth. Conversely, if Mr. Mason is unable to universalize his decision, that is, say that it is appropriate for everyone to do the same thing, then the decision must be immoral.

Kant also asserts that we should not use a person for our own purposes. Both Mr. Maxwell and Mr. Mason would be doing just that. Mr. Maxwell would be doing it to save money and Mr. Mason would be doing it to save his job. If everyone collectively exploited each other this way, each and every person would universally be denied their own humanity. Every person deserves to be treated as a "person" and not as a "thing."

Case Commentary: The Ethic of Justice

Justice ethics requires that we treat each other fairly. Neither Mr. Maxwell nor Mr. Mason would be treating the guests fairly. They would not be treating the employees fairly either if they required them to cheat the guests.

Rawls argues that we can determine what is fair, or just, by determining what rational people, who considered every point of view, would accept as fair. Remember the *veil of ignorance?* It would easily apply in this case. What would Mr. Maxwell do regarding the portion sizes if he did not know where he would wind up in the situation? Would Mr. Maxwell say it is acceptable to cheat the customer if he knew he was to be the customer and not the owner? The same would apply to Mr. Mason.

This case is an example of how crucial certain details can be. A critical fact in this case is that the menu states that the steak is 12 ounces. Reducing the portion size to ten ounces involves defrauding and deceiving the customer. According to some legal applications, the author of a deceptive advertisement must:

1. Intend to have the audience believe something false.

---

[2] Manuel G. Velasquez, *Business Ethics: Concepts and Cases,* 5th ed. (Upper Saddle River, N.J.: Prentice Hall, 2002), p. 362.

2. Know it is false.

3. Deliberately lead the audience into believing the falsehood.[2]

However, consider the differences to our ethical analysis if the menu did not specify the weight of the steak? Would reducing the size of the portion then be ethically permissible? Absolutely. There is no ethical obligation to provide large portions. Deciding to reduce portion size in response to increased costs is perfectly acceptable. What is not ethically permissible is falsely advertising one size and then providing a smaller one. One little detail—advertising a specified size of the portion—makes all the difference.

Retributive justice states that the person who committed the wrong must be aware of what they are doing and freely choose to do it. Second, the person must be aware that what they are doing is wrong. Third, the guilt must be substantiated. Finally, the punishment must match the crime. In this case, both Mr. Maxwell and Mr. Mason are fully aware of what they are doing and they both should know it is wrong. Their guilt would be easy to prove.

A punishment that might properly fit the crime would be a fine levied under the "truth-in-menu" laws. That might be the "institutional punishment" levied against the restaurant, perhaps augmented by public exposure of the misdeed, which could harm future profitability a great deal. Punishment of the two individuals involved is a separate matter. Criminal charges against Maxwell and Mason might be brought under the legal system. An action of this type would be unlikely, unless they were also involved in more widespread fraudulent criminal behavior.

What type of compensatory justice would be proper? If a civil suit were filed, they might be forced to pay back all of the guests whom they cheated. This might be levied as a fine or as community service at a kitchen for the homeless. They certainly would not be jailed for lengthy periods of time because the gravity of the offense would not warrant such a severe punishment.

However, Mr. Maxwell may be considered "more guilty" than Mr. Mason, since he is the ultimate boss. The extenuating circumstances that Mr. Mason is being directly ordered to do the unethical act may make his appropriate punishment a little less severe—but it will not absolve him completely. "I was just following orders," does not absolve one of wrongdoing, if the unethical behavior was done knowingly.

Case Commentary: Aristotle and the Ethics of Virtue

Beyond the morality of the actions, we can also judge each man's character. Aristotle would look at their deceptive behavior and determine that neither Mr. Maxwell nor Mr. Mason has a virtuous character because neither acts the way a human being should act.

Aristotle named four fundamental virtues that are necessary to moral behavior: *courage, temperance, justice and prudence*. Mr. Mason has shown a definite lack of courage because he would not resist Mr. Maxwell. Neither man is exhibiting the virtue of justice. Neither man is showing prudence (wisdom) because they would easily be caught and penalized. Just think how many employees in the kitchen will know that Mr. Mason and Mr. Maxwell are cheating the guests. One's concept of humanity will dictate what that person believes is virtuous. If one believes that honesty is a virtue, one will treat everyone in an honest manner and expect the same in return.

Case Study—Sound Business Practices?

Mary recently graduated with a Masters Degree in hospitality from a prestigious college in the United States. She has been hired as the central purchasing agent for the Manley Arms, a family-owned chain of small, but luxurious, resorts in the British Virgin Islands.

The chain's strategic differentiation from other hotel chains in the immediate area is twofold. First, their concept is all-inclusive, meaning that guests pay only once for all of the main amenities of their stay (lodging, food and beverage, transportation, entertainment, and recreation). Second, the resorts are marketed as the only chain in the Islands that makes available to guests indigenous food and beverage products any day of the week, any time of the day or night. As a result, there is extreme pressure on the purchasing departments of the individual hotels to always have the most popularly requested products (especially local alcoholic beverages) in stock.

There are seven main distilleries and bottlers of local alcoholic beverages in the chain's region. Being a power player in the Islands, Manley Arms has accounts with all seven in order to assure the most competitive pricing.

Every resort, prior to Mary's employ, had a purchasing agent on site who independently received weekly bids from each supplier and then ordered the majority of that week's products from the lowest bidder. Beverage managers at each resort were sent a copy of the week's purchase order so they would know which products the resort would have in stock. The managers ran specials for the week, highlighting drinks made with those products. This system had been in place for the past nine years with very few complaints from either guests or employees.

The owner of the resort expressed interest in opening at least two more resorts over the next three years. He wanted to keep the same operational system, but, given the importance of economies of scale, he also wanted to centralize the purchasing function and eliminate the need for on site purchasing agents. He hired Mary to execute his strategy with both the existing and proposed properties.

None of this information was a secret and word reached the distributors for the distillers and bottlers. Mary was soon flooded with calls and visits. Some came with small "reminders" of their products such as calendars, pens, and wine glasses—all embossed with their companies' logos.

Some representatives arranged for samples so that Mary, along with the company's executive chef and food and beverage director, could taste new product lines. Three representatives of the largest distilleries called Mary's office directly (bypassing both the executive chef and food and beverage director) to arrange private tastings at her home.

At the end of one of these private tastings, the representative left four cases of the company's most expensive wines on Mary's kitchen counter and flatly announced, "I'm sure that we could make this a habit if my company receives the majority of Manley's purchases from now on."

That same weekend, a rather handsome vice president from the most well known bottling company invited Mary to dinner to discuss future business possibilities. His company also had numerous outlets in the United States. During the dinner meeting, the vice president continuously flirted with Mary and she enjoyed the attention. The only discussion of "business" at this two-hour dinner was a conditional offer to hire Mary as an executive in his company after two years—if she made sure that his company received a no-bid contract for all local beers and malt beverages.

The next week, during a meeting with a third company's sales representative (who just happened to be the brother-in-law of the owner's wife) Mary was flatly offered a 10% kick-back on every $1,000 of product ordered from his company during the next six months. He explained that he was retiring soon and that his income was based mainly on commissions.

Mary was thoroughly confused and decided to call a former classmate who she knew attended high school in the British Virgin Islands. The classmate just laughed and said, "Don't sweat it. That's how business is done in the Islands. Just do what's best for you."

Case Questions

1. What are the major ethical issues you find in this case?

2. Is the location, the British Virgin Islands, ethically relevant? Why or why not?

3. If you were Mary, exactly what would you do? Ethically justify your choice of action.

4. Which ethical tradition (utilitarianism, Kantian ethics, Rawlsian justice ethics, or Aristotelian virtue ethics) was most helpful in making your decision about what to do? Explain your answer.

This case was authored by Dwayne Mackey, an international food and beverage business consultant.

Case Study—Stolen Lobster Tails

Munford was the dishwasher at the Heavenly Rest Truck Stop outside of Scranton, Pennsylvania. He had worked there for three months and had just passed his probationary period. He enjoyed the job a great deal, especially when a number of relatives on his wife's side began staying at their home.

Once a month, Heavenly Rest has a special lobster tail dinner. Truckers arrange to make their stop at the Heavenly Rest just so they can have that dinner special. To prepare, the restaurant orders dozens of cases of lobster tails and most of the time they run out before the evening is over.

There was a blizzard on one particular lobster special evening and only about fifty percent of the expected guests showed up. Marvin, the assistant manager, was not too worried because the tails freeze well. He had done it before when inclement weather hit. He knew they would just sell out the next month. He inventoried the tails, noting he had twenty-two full cases.

Later that same evening, during a slight dinner rush, Munford stepped into the freezer to retrieve a bag of ice for one of the servers. He noticed all the leftover lobster tails and thought about what a lovely New Year's Eve dinner they would make for his wife and her extended family who were visiting with them over the winter holiday season.

At the end of the night, while Marvin was finishing up the books in his office, Munford snuck two cases of the lobster tails out to his car. He threw an old blanket over the cases so no one would see his stolen goods.

The next day when Marvin went into the freezer, he immediately realized that two cases of lobster tails were missing. "It's theft, plain and simple," he said to himself. He walked back to his office and shut the door. He wanted to think through the matter without any disturbance.

Marvin soon came to realize that Munford was probably the thief. He decided to approach him and ask him outright. Munford was surprised that he had been so easily caught. He confessed and begged Marvin to give him a second chance. He told him how much he enjoyed the job. He also told Marvin that he was under terrific stress at home with all the visitors.

Case Questions

1. What would you do if you were Marvin? Why?

2. Would your decision be any different if Munford were a 15-year employee with a wonderful work record? Why or why not?

3. Would it change your mind in any way about what should be done with Munford if you found out that Marvin's superior, Jake, the restaurant manager, routinely took home food of equal value to the two cases of lobster tails, and nothing was ever done about it? Why or why not?

Case Study—To Drive or Not to Drive?

Wolf Burger was the night bartender at the Lazy Nights Saloon in Bliston, North Dakota. On this particular evening, Arthur Oakley was sitting at the bar. By 9 p.m., Wolf thought that he had served Arthur one too many drinks and refused to provide him with another.

About fifteen minutes later, Arthur decided to leave the Lazy Nights Saloon. As Arthur was saying his good byes to all his buddies, Wolf thought to himself, "I should not let this guy leave. He's too drunk to drive. And the road conditions are not the best either."

Wolf didn't stop Arthur from leaving. Arthur got in his car and when driving home, he hit another car, killing a family of three: the father, the mother, and their 8-year old son. Arthur was hospitalized with a few broken bones.

Case Questions

1. Who should be held responsible for the deaths? Explain your answer using act and rule utilitarianism, justice ethics, and virtue ethics.

2. What universal rule could be written from this incident?

3. How does the "veil of ignorance" apply to this situation? Explain your answer.

4. If you owned the Lazy Nights Saloon, what policy would you institute that would cover situations like this? Draw up a statement of your policy and justify it as the ethically correct policy.

Case Study—Clean as a Whistle!

Jamie, the executive chef at the Atmore Deluxe Restaurant, was preparing dinner for more than 100 people that evening. There were 75 reservations listed and it was Wednesday, a typically busy night at the restaurant. She had prepped the roasts, given assignments regarding the vegetables and salads, and was now waiting for Rachel, the sous chef, to arrive.

When Rachel walked into the kitchen she looked terrible. She was sneezing and coughing. The chef knew she had to send Rachel home, but she needed her desperately.

Jamie considered her options. "I'll just put Rachel on the cash register, away from food, and bring Carly inside. She is a culinary graduate and she has been dying for a shot at the kitchen." Jamie was satisfied with herself but she knew she was taking a chance. Rachel could still infect people if she was contagious. "I know I should send her home but I need her," she kept thinking. Finally she decided to take a chance.

The dinner went off smoothly; Carly did a wonderful job. Rachel was fine out by the cash register. One of the regular guests came back to the kitchen, as he often did, to thank Jamie. He told her he loved eating at the Atmore because he knew that the kitchen was *clean as a whistle*.

The next day, however, Mr. Gershon, the Atmore's owner, stomped into the restaurant, nearly causing Jamie's soufflé to drop. "What in blazes went on here last night?" he shouted loudly.

Jamie was baffled until she heard Mr. Gershon's explanation. Twenty-two people who had eaten dinner at the Atmore Deluxe Restaurant were hospitalized with Staph Aureus food poisoning early that morning. Jamie immediately knew that Rachel had passed on her infection to guests, probably by handling money.

Case Questions

1. How responsible is Jamie for the food poisoning of the guests? Explain your answer. Is this really a moral issue, or merely a question of good or bad judgment about how sick or contagious someone is? Explain how you came to your conclusion.

2. What is the ethically right thing to do now? Nothing, or something? If something, what? Ethically justify your answer.

Case Study—Ratting

Alex Robertson was a line cook at Josephine's Fine Dining, a high-priced restaurant located in Lincoln, Nebraska. One night while Alex was on a break, he stepped out to the back alley and found his friend Mike Norman, a fellow line cook, smoking marijuana. Mike offered some pot to Alex. Mike told Alex that he smoked pot almost every night because it made the time go faster.

Alex politely refused, but when he did so, Mike asked him not to "rat" on him. They both knew it was against company policy and cause for immediate dismissal. Alex promised not to turn him in because Mike was not only a good friend, but also a very good co-worker.

A week later, the restaurant manager, Brandon Richman, called Alex into his office. He told Alex that he heard rumors that kitchen employees were smoking marijuana while on the job. He asked Alex if he knew of any such doings. Brandon also asked Alex if he knew who could be doing it.

Alex felt like a deer caught in the headlights. He tried to think clearly. He considered himself a good friend, but he also considered himself an exemplary employee. He made a quick decision. He said, "I'll keep my eyes peeled for any wrong-doing, Mr. Richman."

Two weeks later, Brandon Richman found out who had been smoking marijuana, and also who was covering up for him. He planned to fire Mike immediately because he had proof of his pot smoking at work. Even though he was fully aware that Alex did not smoke marijuana while at work, he decided to fire him anyway in order to make an example to the other employees.

Case Questions

1. What would you have done in Alex's place when Mike asked him not to "rat?" What is the ethically correct thing to do? Explain your answer.

2. What are the ethical issues involved?

3. Was Alex's behavior ethical? Explain your answer.

4. Was Mike's behavior ethical? Explain your answer

5. Did Brandon Richman make an ethical decision? Explain your answer.

Case Study—Tip Reporting

Freddy was a waiter at the London Port Steak House in Greenwich. He earned over $150 a night in tips, as well as a small salary. He knew that he was required by the Internal Revenue Service to report those tips. However, Freddy did not think it was fair that he should have to pay taxes on his tips; he felt that the restaurant ought to pay those taxes for him.

Consequently, Freddy reported only $25 per night. Mr. Quinlan, his immediate supervisor at the restaurant, knew that Freddy was being dishonest about his tip reporting. But Mr. Quinlan felt it was Freddy's responsibility, not his, to ensure that the IRS got its due.

As luck would have it, Freddy was audited that year. He immediately went to Mr. Quinlan, his supervisor, telling him about his woes with the Internal Revenue Service and asking for assistance.

"Would you please back me up about the $25 per night? I'll make it worth your while in the future," he added.

Case Questions

1. If you were Mr. Quinlan, what exactly would you do? Explain why.

2. Evaluate the ethics of misreporting your income to the federal government in order to pay fewer taxes. List arguments that could be made stating that is acceptable and list the counter arguments stating that it is not acceptable.

Case Study—Your Heart's Delight

June was a regular customer at the Heart's Delight Restaurant and Delicatessen. June always celebrated her birthday at Heart's Delight so everyone knew she was 80 years old. She ate at the restaurant twice a week, usually on Mondays and Thursdays. She always ordered the daily specials and took home more than half of the meal as a take-out. Then, like clockwork, every Friday, June returned her mostly eaten leftovers, claiming that they were spoiled by the time she got home.

Everyone at the restaurant knew that June has reduced economic circumstances and the countermen always gave her something to take home for the weekend to "replace" the leftovers.

After the new manager, Bryce Higgins, saw this happen twice, he approached Michael, the counterman, and asked him what was going on. Michael explained the circumstances and was quite surprised to hear Bryce say that no one was to give June "replacement" food any longer.

Case Questions

1. What are the ethical issues in this case?

2. What would you do if you were the manager of Heart's Delight? Why? Explain your answer using act and rule utilitarianism, justice ethics, and virtue ethics.

Case Study—Something for Nothing

Jack Moss and his friend Joanne were dining at *Le Fleur,* one of the newest, upscale establishments in Dayton, Ohio. Jack had offered to take Joanne out for a fine dining experience to celebrate their newly formed partnership.

Toward the end of the meal, Jack slipped a tiny piece of glass from his jacket pocket onto his plate (Joanne saw him do it but Jack did not know that Joanne had seen him). Jack immediately called the waiter, Bryan, over to the table. In a whisper

Jack told him to look on his plate. Jack pointed directly at the glass and asked to see the manager immediately.

Bryan agreed to get the manager, but, unbeknownst to Jack, Bryan had also seen Jack slip the glass onto the plate. Bryan found the manager, Ms. Baum, in the kitchen under very harried circumstances. One of the chefs had to be sent home due to illness and orders were backed up in the kitchen. Ms. Baum was doing her best to assist.

As quickly as possible, Bryan explained the situation to Ms. Baum, including the fact that the guest had slipped the glass onto his own plate. Ms. Baum left the kitchen to speak with Jack. Jack insisted that the dinners should be complementary because of the glass. When Ms. Baum did not immediately agree, Jack started to raise his voice and started causing a disturbance in the otherwise very quiet dining room. Guests began looking in their direction; Ms. Baum was mortified and tried to get control of the situation.

Case Questions

1. What are all of the ethical issues in this case? Explain your answer.

2. What would you do if you were Joanne? Explain your answer.

3. What would you do if you were Ms. Baum? Explain your answer.

4. Apply each of the ethical theories we have studied to this case. Explain each of your applications.

Applying Ethics to the Hotel Front Office Function

T HE FRONT OFFICE is the most visible department in a hotel and the focal point of the front office is the front desk. The front desk is the hub of any hotel, whether a small roadside operation or a five-star luxury resort. Often, the first encounter a guest has with a hotel is with the front desk staff. Guests come to the front desk to register, to receive room assignments, to obtain information about services, facilities, and the community, and to settle their accounts and check out. Whenever problems or questions arise, guests generally pick up the phone and call the front desk. Front desk employees have a great deal of influence and responsibility. They need to know who to contact for the various problems that arise.

Front office operations cover more than just the interactions at the front desk. Functions include reservations, communications (telephone switchboard), uniformed service, and security responsibilities. Money can be a very powerful motivator to engage in unethical behavior. Many hotels average hundreds of cash and credit card transactions each day, giving rise to opportunities for theft and other unethical behavior. Other areas of concern may arise in relation to a property's reservation practices (overbooking), employees overcharging for services, violations of guest privacy, and many other situations.

The case below, "Things Go Bump in the Night," addresses overbooking and is followed by ethical analyses in relation to utilitarianism, Kant's categorical imperative, Rawls's justice ethics, and Aristotle's ethics of virtue. The chapter closes with a series of case studies and questions about the cases that challenge you to analyze ethical issues that arise in front office operations.

Case Study—Things Go Bump in the Night

> Two weeks before her niece's wedding, Esther Barnes negotiated a room rate with the Panda Bear Inn. She received a reservation confirmation number for a double room for two people for two nights. When Esther and her husband arrived at the Panda Bear Inn, much to their dismay, they were told that their room was not available because the Inn had overbooked and they would be put up in a different hotel only five miles away.
>
> They had been traveling most of the day and were very tired. Mrs. Barnes felt a little better when she was told that the Panda Bear Inn would pay for the room at the Lion's Gate Inn. Driving another

five miles didn't seem too much of an inconvenience. However, when the front desk manager told her that the Panda Bear Inn would not host the Barnes' for the two nights at Lion's Gate, she became a little irritated. The manager further explained that Panda Bear Inn had openings for the second night and the Barnes' would have to return to the Inn for the second night.

Since Esther wanted to retain the room rate she had negotiated, she agreed and the Barnes' left to stay at the Lion's Gate for their first night in town. After checking in at the Lions' Gate, they had to completely unpack and ready their clothes for the morning breakfast at her sister's house. The next day, they had to leave the family function and return to the Lion's Gate, repack their belongings, check out, and drive to the Panda Bear Inn. Once there, they again checked in, unpacked, and rushed to get ready for the late afternoon ceremony and the evening reception.

The next morning Esther and her husband felt like they spent more of their time packing and unpacking than they did visiting and celebrating with their relatives. During their trip home, Esther told her husband that their experience reminded her of getting bumped off a flight by an airline—but, in this case, they were not compensated for their inconvenience. She also questioned the legality of overbooking. She quipped, "What good is a confirmation number, when there is no guarantee of a room?" Esther decided to write a letter to the corporate headquarters of the Panda Bear Inn hotel chain.

Do no-shows and late cancellations justify overbooking? Do the operational advantages of overbooking outweigh the inconvenience to guests? Were the Barnes' treated properly? How would you feel if this happened to you?

Consider an analogous situation. Imagine going to your hair stylist for a late Tuesday afternoon appointment. You expect to be there for two hours. You are very excited because that evening you are going to an important business function where you will meet many significant people in your field. However, when you arrive, you are told that Eva, your favorite hair stylist, is overbooked and the salon has arranged for you to have your hair done at the XYZ Salon, a half hour away. They explained to you that Tuesdays average three cancellations, so the salon always overbooks. On your Tuesday, however, there were no cancellations. Would you consider this acceptable behavior on the part of the salon?

Case Commentary: Utilitarianism

The act utilitarian point of view on the Barnes's situation asks, "Was the greatest good achieved for the greatest number of people?" Possibly—the only ones inconvenienced were Mr. and Mrs. Barnes. The hotel owners certainly achieved their greatest good, at least in the short run. They made the most money possible by having sold all the rooms. However, allowing guests to think their rooms are guaranteed when they really are not, may have numerous harmful consequences for the hotel owners, both short term and long term. The corporation is using the guest to achieve the highest possible profit for that day, while paying less attention to the guest's needs and comfort.

What are the consequences if a hotel develops a reputation for consistently overbooking? What are the consequences if employees see overbooking as management's inconsiderate treatment of guests? Employees often take their cue from their supervisors. The housekeeper might decide that the bathroom looks "clean enough" for guests. The bellperson might decide to charge a guest for calling a taxi.

An act utilitarian considers *all of the consequences* of the action. There are also consequences to never overbooking: lost revenue for the hotel owners and empty rooms denied to travelers in need of lodging.

For act utilitarianism, deciding the morality of action involves a balancing act: you weigh the total benefits against the total harms likely to result from a specific act. You are ethically obligated to undertake the action that results in the *greatest net benefit* for all concerned.

In the case of overbooking, the many factors you must balance can make the calculation fairly complicated. If a hotel only overbooks by X percent of rooms, and the X percent overbooking rate very seldom results in any guest being "walked," the net harm is relatively small. Since the benefits of a full hotel are many, act utilitarianism may find this level of overbooking ethically acceptable, because the benefits outweigh the harms.

However, it is also a question of how injurious the harms are. If a guest denied a room because of overbooking is greatly harmed (forced to travel a great distance for alternative accommodations, or forced to accept inferior accommodations, etc.), then the weight may swing in the direction of making overbooking unethical. Another factor that would affect the balance (and, hence, the morality of overbooking) is how much overbooking is practiced. If, instead of X percent of rooms being overbooked, three times X percent are overbooked, and this higher rate means that guests are frequently denied the rooms they reserved, then the amount of harm increases significantly. Thus, act utilitarianism may condone a certain level of overbooking but not higher levels. It is all a matter of examining the amount of benefit and harm done, and choosing the course of action most likely to maximize the net benefit for all concerned.

Rule utilitarianism applies the principle of "greatest good" to rules of conduct, not to individual acts. So the question is: can a rule allowing overbooking be morally justified? It is apparent that rules allowing frequent denial of reserved service would not produce "the greatest happiness for the greatest number," and thus they would be considered unethical. But it is quite possible that "mild" forms of overbooking, those that result in very few denials of reserved service and/or in small inconveniences, would be judged ethically acceptable.

Case Commentary: Kant's Categorical Imperative

Kant would view overbooking differently from the utilitarian perspective. He would be primarily concerned with the individual rights of the person denied what they were promised. If the hotel had overbooked because there had been a natural disaster in the area and they were trying to accommodate as many people as possible, Kant would maintain that this might be acceptable because of the motive behind the action. The overbooking was done out of a sense of duty to one's fellow man; it, therefore, may be the right thing to do. However from a Kantian ethical perspective, it would be much harder to justify overbooking as a routine business practice ensuring higher daily profits.

Consider the two formulations of Kant's *categorical imperative* that we have studied. First, we should act in a way that whatever rule we follow, we could will this to be a universal rule. Since a reservation is a promise to deliver a service (room, airline flight, etc.), denial of that service is breaking a promise. As with all forms of promising, Kant would condemn breaking the promise because breaking promises destroys the very basis of making a promise in the first place. It is self-contradictory to make a promise and break that promise; hence it is irrational and immoral. Thus, the first formulation of Kant's categorical imperative would condemn any overbooking that actually resulted in the denial of a promised service.

The second form of the categorical imperative stipulates that one must not use people for his or her own purposes. On the face of it, the practice of overbooking appears to do just that. Guests are used to ensure higher profits for the corporations without regard for the humanity or autonomy of those guests. Essentially, the guest has been "used" because he or she was, in effect, lied to when the reservation was made.

To illustrate this, consider the following situation. You arrive at your destination hotel after ten very long hours of traveling including a number of airplane changes, delays, bad weather, and lost luggage—only to find out that your room reservation was not honored. Imagine that you had guaranteed your late arrival and even called just a few hours earlier and were assured a room. Now imagine that you have to taxi to another location and you have the further inconvenience of informing the airline to deliver your lost luggage to this other destination. Would you feel used? Would you have been degraded from the status of a human being to that of a "thing" used for someone else's convenience?

There may be, however, another way that overbooking could be made compatible with Kantian ethics. If the guest or passenger is made aware, *at the time the reservation is made,* that a "reservation" does not actually guarantee a room or flight, only a very high likelihood of its availability, then no promise has been made. No deception would have occurred in the event of denial of "reserved" service. The guest or passenger would not have been "used" because he or she was aware in advance that there is at least a slight possibility of denial of service. He or she would then be able to rationally make a decision about what to do, and no deception or denial of humanity has occurred.

These appear to be the only circumstances where Kant would find overbooking to be morally acceptable. This is an example of a practice where Kantian ethics is much stricter than utilitarian ethics, which may find overbooking ethically acceptable in a larger number of circumstances than would Kant.

Case Commentary: The Ethic of Justice

Justice ethics states that we should treat each other fairly and asks us to look at the situation from behind the *veil of ignorance.* Imagine that you do not know if you were to be the front desk manager (who earns a bonus based on profit and daily occupancy rates) or if you were to be the weary traveler who discovers that the "guaranteed" room reservation was, in fact, not guaranteed. If everyone involved in making the decision were both rational and interested in their own well being, many of the more permissive forms of overbooking would not be tolerated. A rational person would set up rules protecting the interests of the traveler, since he or she may end up being that traveler. Even if mild forms of overbooking were to be allowed, a justice ethic would place strong and effective restrictions on the practice.

Compensatory justice would also dictate that the wronged guest must be compensated for the loss and inconvenience. Some suggest that a guest might expect a free night at a nearby hotel of the same or better quality, a free phone call to notify friends or family of the hotel change, and a free upgrade on a future visit. Is this enough compensation for the traveler? Is this fair to the traveler? What if the person never expects to be in the area again? What good would the future upgrade do? In considering what is fair, you must ask questions such as: what has the hotel lost and what has the guest lost? What is the compensation costing the hotel? What is the denial of a room costing the potential guest?

Case Commentary: Aristotle and the Ethics of Virtue

Virtue ethics would view the hotel as a human community and ask how well does the hotel contribute to the development of the character traits of its employees? The traits or virtues include honesty, integrity, tolerance, fairness, and cooperation. Overbooking raises concerns about how well a hotel fosters honesty, integrity, and fairness if it does not keep its word to its guests. Any enterprise that engages in overbooking needs to be sure that this practice is honest and open and it does not promote an ethic of deception or irresponsibility in its employees. Virtue ethics requires businesses to foster values that relate to the way it interacts with its community. A business has to display a solid ethical culture in order to be respected by its community.

Case Study—The Wedding Party

For the past five years, Hadley Greerson has been the front desk manager at the Eternal Bliss Hotel in Perpetual City. Previously, she had been the assistant front desk manager at the Honeymoon Heaven Hotel in the adjacent town of Andover.

More than a decade ago, the Eternal Bliss Hotel became recognized as a premier honeymoon spot. It is one of the many well-known honeymoon hotels in this area of the country. At least one wedding is held at the hotel each weekend all year long. The honeymoon couple often stays at least a few days after the wedding. The hotel has 300 guestrooms, six honeymoon suites, and eight ballrooms.

Amanda and Hal Butts have just arrived from Andover. They are in the bridal party for Rose and Richard Wooster, a wedding that is to take place in the hotel that evening. Jill Everley, the front desk agent on duty at Eternal Bliss, welcomes Amanda and Hal to the hotel. Jill has only been working at this hotel for just under a year. The Butts ask to have the keys to the room of the bridal couple. They want to leave champagne, flowers, and hors d'oeuvres in the bridal suite.

Jill knows the policy of the hotel. She is not allowed to give out room numbers of guests, let alone keys to guestrooms or bridal suites. Politely, Jill informs the Butts that she cannot give them the keys.

The Butts persist and argue persuasively. They point out that the couple hasn't even checked in yet. If only they are given the keys, anyone on the hotel staff can come with them and check everything out that they do. In fact, they insist the hotel can help, and they are willing to pay anybody who is willing to assist them.

Case Questions

1. What would you do if you were Jill Everley? Why?

2. If you were Hadley Greerson, and you became aware of the request, how would you handle it? List all the things that you would do and explain why you would do them.

3. Can you think of any differences in what a utilitarian, a Kantian, a Rawlsian (justice), or an Aristotelian (virtue) would tell Jill or Hadley to do? Explain your answer.

Case Study—Nobody Will Ever Know

John Flowers is the senior stylist at Happy Locks Salon located on property at the Marvella Resort, near Pensacola, Florida. Mr. Flowers recently approached Ms. Sheila Meriwether about lowering the monthly rent on his salon space, as business had been slow in recent months. Ms. Meriwether denied his request adding that they did not raise his rent during other months when Mr. Flowers was busier than usual. She also told him that the salon was slow in general and they needed the income for overhead expenses.

Since Mr. Flowers felt that his work was in great demand at the Marvella, he assumed that he should go over Ms. Meriwether's head and speak with the hotel's general manager, Esther Soloff. Mrs. Soloff was sympathetic to Mr. Flowers but also insisted that they would not lower his rent.

Mr. Flowers was not happy. He was determined to earn at least another $50 per week. Later that evening, he broached the subject with Evan, his friend who was on the night shift at the Marvella front desk. Evan was also sympathetic but said to John, "Look, it's tough all over but you'll just have to bite the bullet. It will get busy again. In the meantime, maybe you can cry a little to your best customers and squeeze out a bit more in tips."

John started to object, but then he got a gleam in his eye. He thought Evan's remarks over and said, "You know, Evan, you may just have something there." And he walked away with a bounce, looking much happier than he did earlier.

I wonder what he's up to, Evan thought to himself.

Three months later, Evan was at the front desk when the phone rang. It was Mrs. Hoolihan, a very irate customer. She demanded to speak to the general manager immediately.

"I'm sorry, ma'am, she's not here. Can I help you in any way?" Evan asked in a very understanding tone of voice.

"Who are you? Are you a manager of some type?" Mrs. Hoolihan asked.

"My name is Evan, ma'am and I manage complaints in the evening."

"Well, I certainly have a complaint young man. I received my credit card bill and your hotel overcharged me."

"I'm sure I can help you with that. How exactly were you overcharged?"

"In the salon. I had my hair colored, cut, and blown dry. It came to a total of $125. I still have the receipt. But the charge from the Happy Locks Salon is for $135. I am furious young man. Money does not grow on trees, you know!"

Evan pulled up the account history and immediately saw the problem. A tip of $10 had been added to the charge. He casually asked Mrs. Hoolihan about a tip and she told him that she distinctly remembers that she gave the stylist a cash tip of $10. "I would have given him more, but all he did was whine about money. I did not like that at all," she added.

Evan assured her that he would credit the $10 to her charge card. After he hung up, he looked over other salon fees and he began to discern a pattern. He remembered the conversation he had with John Flowers. He suspected that John was helping himself to the customer's money. If that was true, he knew it was outright theft. He decided he would talk to John first before reporting the discrepancy. However, when he spoke to John, the stylist did not even deny it. He rationalized that the salon was taking too much money and he was getting the clients to "chip in" on his salon space rental.

Evan told him that he would have to stop immediately and John agreed. "Are you going to report me?" John asked Evan. "It was only a couple hundred dollars, you know."

Case Questions

1. Explain John's rationalization from a utilitarian point of view.

2. How would Kant view this situation? Use the categorical imperative to explain your answer.

3. If you were Evan, what would you do? Which ethical theory (utilitarianism, Kantian ethics, Rawlsian justice, or Aristotelian virtue ethics) was most helpful in making your decision about what to do?

Case Study—Front Desk Politics

Three young women have been working at the Devil's Rock Inn, a popular conference and banquet spot, located in a beautiful country-like setting. Molly is a front desk agent, Jane is a banquet salesperson, and Sue is in charge of the marketing and sales department.

In the past, whenever banquet information requests came to the front desk, Molly always forwarded them to Jane because Jane gets a full commission when she handles the requests directly. A month ago, Jane embarrassed Molly at an office event and Molly has been angry with her ever since. Now, she automatically forwards the requests to Sue in marketing and sales. Sue assigns one of her staff members to follow up. When the information finally does get to Jane, she only receives half of the commission she would earn if the request went to her first. She now has to split the commission with one of Sue's staff members.

Molly has two reasons for re-routing the requests. Not only is she still angry with Jane, but she also wants to get a job in Sue's department. She appreciates how Sue treats her employees and also she knows she will make more money once she gets into marketing and sales.

Case Questions

1. Are there any ethical issues involved? If so, what are they? Explain your answer.

2. Is Molly treating Jane in an unethical manner? Or, is this just a case of office politics?

3. If you were the assistant manager, overseeing all of these employees, would you see the situation as merely a practical question to solve without ethical consequences? Or, would you find yourself involved with ethical issues? Explain your answer.

Case Study—Always Read the Small Print

The management at the Dover Inn adds fifteen percent to every hotel gift shop purchase when it is charged to a guest's room. The policy is noted only on the guest's final bill at check-out time. Most guests do not notice the charge and just pay their bill. The hotel profits by several hundred dollars a week from this covert policy.

Moreover, gift shop employees are instructed to encourage shoppers to charge their purchases to their guestrooms. It is suggested that salespeople ask, "For your convenience, would you like me to charge this to your room?"

Front desk agents are mandated to remove the additional fees if a guest complains. At check-out time, Mrs. Kramer noticed the additional charge on her bill. She very politely asked Ellen, the front desk agent, what the additional charge was for. Ellen, just as politely, explained the policy, showing Mrs. Kramer the small print.

Mrs. Kramer became incensed. She demanded that the charges be removed immediately. She also said that she was going to send a report of this to her three favorite Internet travel sites. She also insisted on seeing the general manager and told him that aside from the Internet sites, she was going to write a letter to all of the local newspapers in the region.

Case Questions

1. What ethical issues are involved with the Dover Inn's policy? What would you advise the general manager to do? Explain your answer.

2. What ethical issues are involved for all of the employees concerned? What would you advise the front desk employees? The shop employees? Explain your answers.

Case Study—The Safety Sheet

Rebecca, the front desk agent at the Goodfriend Inn, was told to hand out a safety sheet with each room key that she distributed. However, she found that the safety sheet (which details safety precautions in case of fire, hurricane, electrical failure, and more) was upsetting to most of the guests. She decided to stop handing out the sheet, except when a supervisor was around.

Case Questions

1. What are the ethical issues in this case? Explain your answer?

2. What would Kant say about this case? Explain your answer.

3. What would a utilitarian say about this case? Explain your answer.

4. What would you do if you were Rebecca? Why?

Case Study—Who Are You Anyway?

Peter is the morning shift front desk agent at Roger's Roadside Motel. The Roger's Motel chain has grown rapidly in recent years and now, due to its excellent reputation for both great service and cleanliness, it has 62 sites around the United States.

Periodically, Peter pilfers guest credit card information. He uses two criteria for his selection process. He chooses someone he thinks would not notice additional charges on their credit card statement or he chooses someone he thinks would not know what to do if they did get overcharged on their bill.

Peter does not use the credit card information himself. He sells the information to Jack, a friend of his; who in turn, sells it to Christopher, who sells it over the Internet for identity theft purposes. Their identity theft ring has been going on for well over two years.

Gerald, the General Manger, recently got wind of the theft. He did not have specific proof until just a few days ago when he asked his friend, Gertie, to check into the hotel and stay a few days. He instructed Gertie to act as absentmindedly as she possibly could. Gertie had fun with the undercover work. When her credit card statement arrived at the end of the month, she found several minor charges totaling about $150. Each charge was so minor that she had trouble spotting them.

Gerald was in a quandary. He knew he had to fire Peter. He also knew he had to break up this identity theft ring. But, he did not want to involve the local police. He was afraid that the bad publicity would be ruinous to the business; he was sure that guests would be afraid to come to the hotel. But, he also believed that justice should be served.

Case Questions

1. What would you do if you were Gerald? Explain your answer.

2. What would a utilitarian say about the situation? Explain your answer.

3. What would Kant say about the situation? Explain your answer.

4. What would Aristotle say about the situation? Explain your answer.

Case Study—Blowing the Whistle

Pablo has been a front desk employee at Odell's Roadside Inn for four years. He has a lot of responsibility for a front desk agent and he is paid extra for it. This particular Odell's is one of 22 inns started by the Odell family in 1955.

Victor is the front desk manager. He has worked for the Odell's chain since he graduated from college in 1996. He enjoys his job very much. Recently, he bought a new convertible sports car, which he likes to talk about to anyone who will listen.

Four months ago, Pablo noticed something strange when he did the night audit. He knew that room 222 had been rented for that night because he had made the reservation himself. However, it showed up on the audit as vacant. Over the next month, Pablo watched for further inaccuracies, and he found a minimum of one per week. He realized that someone was pocketing cash at the owner's expense.

He called his friend Wade who was also a front desk agent with night audit responsibilities for Odell's. Wade and Pablo had been friends for a long time and Pablo felt comfortable discussing the situation with Wade. They decided not to say anything but to keep watching. Wade was going to pay special attention at his hotel, too.

During the next month, they realized that there was a scam going on and that it probably affected other Odell properties as well. Neither one of them wanted to "blow the whistle." Both of them liked their jobs and neither of them wanted to tattle.

Case Questions

1. What should Pablo and Wade do? Discuss at least two or three alternatives. Which one would you select?

2. Assume that Pablo spoke to a regional manager about what he knew and the very next day Victor fired him with no explanation. As far as Victor can see, nothing will be done. Now, what should Wade do? Explain your answer.

3. Analyze the situation in question #2 from a utilitarian point of view and from a Kantian "rights" point of view. What does each analysis tell you should be done and by whom? Explain your answer.

Case Study—Lady of the Night?

Ethan is the front desk agent at the Harbor Inn in Fort Lauderdale, Florida. He has worked the front desk for two years, while completing his college degree in hotel management. Ethan noticed that Adrienne Shaw, a guest that checked in a week ago, left the hotel several times each night and returned with a different man. He strongly suspects some type of prostitution.

Case Questions

1. What are the ethical issues involved in this case? Explain your answer.

2. Apply each of the ethical theories we have studied to this case. Explain each of your applications.

3. What would you do if you were Ethan? Explain your answer.

Case Study—"But What Happened to My Room?"

Liz Borden arrived at the Savoy Hotel at 9 P.M. on a very snowy night. She did not have a reservation but did not expect to have trouble getting a room.

Paige Lewis was the front desk agent. She had been with the Savoy for six months and enjoyed her job very much. Her supervisor, Claire, was pleased with her work and told her so often.

Liz explained her situation to Paige, but the hotel was completely booked. Liz was very upset. She was especially upset at the thought of going out into the snow again searching for a room.

"You don't really think all of the guests will show tonight, do you? I mean, look at that snow out there. Surely people are stopping as soon as possible. And," she added in a conspiratorial tone, "you don't want me to have to go back out there. Just look at it!"

Indeed, it was snowing hard. Paige thought to herself, "There probably would be a guest or two who did not show. But, also, I know the policy of the Savoy: *Honor the reservations at all cost.*"

Just as Paige was about to say "No" once again, she noticed a $50 bill in Liz's hand. "This is yours if you manage to find me a room," Liz said. Paige found a room for Liz.

Just before midnight, a harried young woman with her small child came in from the snow. "I have a reservation," she said.

But, her room was gone. There were no rooms left at the Savoy. When she was told that there had been some mistake and there were no rooms left, she said, "But what happened to my room?"

Case Questions

1. What are all of the ethical issues involved in this case? Explain your answer.

2. Apply each of the ethical theories we have studied to this case. Explain each of your applications.

3. If you were Claire's supervisor, and discovered what Paige had done, what would you do?

10

Ethics and the Human Resources Management Function

Human resources management encompasses a wide range of topics as it deals with how people in the workplace treat one another. This chapter focuses on ethical issues relating to four areas: compensation, diversity, employee treatment (for example sexual harassment, fair and equal treatment in the workplace), and working conditions.

Human resources management is, simply put, *the administration and supervision of the people in the workplace.* Human beings would like to be treated with consideration, respect, and dignity. They would like to be treated fairly. The human resources department in a hospitality organization is given both the responsibility and oversight regarding treatment of employees. It has the very important task of balancing efficiency with equity. If the department can succeed in attaining this equilibrium, management will most likely enjoy a smoothly run operation. Employees who are well treated tend to be loyal to an organization. Loyalty ensures low turnover, which can provide stability to any company.

Many of the theorists we have studied discuss equitable treatment of people. Kantian moral philosophy focuses on respect for the rights of human beings. John Rawls's concept of justice concerns fair and just treatment. Aristotle's virtue ethics looks at moral character in one's dealings with others. And utilitarianism looks for a balance in achieving the greatest good for the greatest number of people.

The case below, "Salary Disclosure," is followed by ethical analyses in relation to utilitarianism, Kant's categorical imperative, Rawls's justice ethics, and Aristotle's ethics of virtue. The chapter closes with a series of case studies and questions about the cases that challenge you to analyze ethical issues that arise in human resources management.

Case Study—Salary Disclosure

The Jensen Hotel has an unwritten policy that forbids employees to discuss their salaries with one another. It recently came to the attention of Dan Maloney, the front desk manager, that George and Barbara, two front desk agents, had compared salaries. Barbara and George have worked at the Jensen Hotel for about a year. By all accounts, the quantity and quality of their work has been essentially the same. However, Barbara found that she earns less than George, even though she does the same work and they were hired at about the same time.

Barbara approached Dan, wanting him to intercede on her behalf with Mr.Grey, the hotel manager. She told him that she would like her salary adjusted to George's level.

Dan explained to Barbara that even though she was doing the same job, she did not have the same experience as George. George had been in the hotel industry for more than five years, while Barbara had only recently graduated from college. He also told her that George had a family to support while she did not.

The foremost issue in this case is a possible discriminatory compensation policy. Therefore, the principal human resources issue we have to consider is fairness. Is it fair to pay two people different salaries for doing the same work? This is both a legal and an ethical question. Many forms of discrimination that are considered unfair have been made illegal in the employment relationship. Beyond the legal ramifications, ethical and practical considerations show that it is unwise for a business enterprise to engage in human resources practices that are considered unfair.

Case Commentary: Utilitarianism

Utilitarianism claims that an action is moral if it maximizes benefits and minimizes harm. In this case, one of the potential benefits to the hotel might be a budgetary savings achieved by paying Barbara less than George, even though they do equivalent work. Shortsighted supervisors might look at their labor budgets and think just that. However, this type of thinking might do more harm than good. Many other consequences become apparent when we look more closely at the matter.

Many criteria can be used in deciding compensation: equality, effort, productivity skills, need, etc. However, in the United States, most claim to adhere to the principle of "equal pay for equal work." In our case, since equal pay is not being given, a crucial question is whether there is equal work. Is Barbara performing as well as George? In other cases this might be an issue, but in our case everybody agrees that George and Barbara are roughly equivalent in performance. Consequently, by not paying the same for similar quantity and quality of work, Maloney and Grey are breaching a widely accepted principle of the society. Violating acknowledged principles of fairness and justice usually leads to other consequences, many of them negative for all concerned.

Unequal pay for equal work could demoralize the workforce, which, in turn, could lead to instability and turnover. The costs of turnover in a front desk position could be as high as $10,000—if we consider the expenses of training a new person, which involves pay for both the trainer and the trainee in addition to human resources management's time in selecting the new staff member. Furthermore, consider the cost of the lower productivity that would result from a new hire. A new trainee will not work at the same level or speed as an experienced employee.

Coworkers and supervisors would have to assist the new hire and, therefore, the cost of their additional work would have to be calculated, as well.

What is the balance of benefits to harm? If not paying people equally for equal work leads to a demoralized workforce, the harm will surely outweigh the benefit. If Mr. Maloney and Mr. Grey consider salaries from a utilitarian perspective, they might well conclude that any savings from Barbara's lower salary are far outweighed by the harm done by violating a widely held principle of justice.

Additionally, Mr. Maloney, on behalf of the hotel, had prohibited the front desk employees from discussing their salaries, thinking that this would head off any discontent caused by salary discrepancies. However, as it happens, the policy is illegal according to the National Labor Relations Act (NLRA). Section 8 of the NLRA specifically states:

> *It shall be an unfair labor practice for an employer . . . to interfere with, restrain, or coerce employees in the exercise of the rights guaranteed in section 7 (one of which is 'to engage in other concerted activities').*[1]

Employees are unable to engage in concerted activities if they cannot talk to each other. Therefore, any type of dialogue between employees about wages or other terms and conditions of employment cannot be barred from discussion as long as it does not interfere with their work. The "no salary discussion" policy of Mr. Grey and Mr. Maloney is illegal and cannot be enforced. If it is unethical to break the law, the unethical behavior belongs to Maloney and Grey, not to Barbara and George when they compared salaries.

In summation, it appears that paying employees equally for equal performance is the ethical thing to do according to a utilitarian perspective. In addition, prohibiting employees from discussing salaries is illegal and, therefore, is likely to lead to more harm than good.

Case Commentary: Kant's Categorical Imperative

Kant would ask if the rule or principle that is being used to determine compensation can be turned into a universal principle without becoming self-contradictory. "Equal pay for equal work" could easily be universalized, but what principle is being used by Mr. Maloney and Mr. Grey? If there is no principle, and they are simply arbitrarily assigning Barbara a lower pay because they think they can get away with it, their actions cannot be ethically justified. On the other hand, if they are employing a universal principle such as "those with a larger family will be paid more," or "greater experience will be progressively rewarded with higher pay," they may be able to come up with an *ethically* defensible justification for their action, even if that action may be practically indefensible or unworkable within the context of the United States legal system. The moral key for Kant would be that universal rules respecting the humanity and autonomy of all be followed. In this

---

[1] *National Labor Relations Act (1935)*, sections 7–8.

case, it is not clear that these kinds of universal rules are applied; but if they are, no moral offense has occurred.

Kant would also want to know if the rule prohibiting employees from speaking to each other about salaries violates the equal liberty of all to live and act as autonomous, rational human beings. If the rule treats adult human beings as children unable to reason for themselves, or if it degrades their humanity because they are being "used," Kant would find the rule to be a violation of the second formulation of the *categorical imperative* (always treat humanity as an end, never as a mere means).

On the face of it, Kant would probably consider the order to conceal salaries degrading. Kant's categorical imperative states that human beings have a clear interest in freedom from fraud and freedom to think, associate, and speak as they choose.[2] These rights can be prohibited only if we agree that we are willing to prohibit everyone from these same rights. Consequently, we can infer that Kant would declare that the supervisors were not giving full autonomy to the employees. Based on Kant's categorical imperative, we see that the supervisors are taking away the employees' decision-making power. It is perfectly acceptable for George to decide not to discuss his salary with Barbara. However, in that case, it is George's decision. He has the choice to act in a free and autonomous manner. Kant's main objective is to assure that people are being treated like human beings and not as "things." Anything that threatens our special moral status as human beings contradicts the Kantian perspective.

Case Commentary: The Ethic of Justice

John Rawls would ask all of the players in the case to step behind the *veil of ignorance*. What salary arrangement would Mr. Grey suggest if he did not know where he was to wind up in the situation? Would he be the front desk agent who is being paid less? Would he be the general manager? Or, would he be one of the other staff members in the scenario? The same goes for Dan Maloney, the front desk manager. It even would hold true for George, the higher paid front desk employee. None of them would wish to be the lower paid front desk agent. Therefore, if they would not want to see themselves in that situation, ethically speaking, they should not want to see someone else in those circumstances either.

Rawls proposes that economic inequality is acceptable only if it is to the greatest benefit for the least advantaged person in the situation. In our case, Barbara is the least advantaged person. Rawls would only consider the lower salary acceptable if it could be proven that she was receiving a higher salary because of this inequality than she would end up with if she were paid the same as George (e.g., if the equal pay were so harmful that the hotel had to lay her off and alternative jobs paid less than her current one).

Rawls's principle of equal liberty includes, among other rights, the right to freedom of speech. While management is, of course, allowed to restrict certain

---

[2] Manuel G. Velasquez, *Business Ethics: Concepts and Cases,* 5th ed. (Upper Saddle River, N.J.: Prentice Hall, 2002), p. 101.

kinds of speech (disruptive, slanderous, damaging to reputation, etc.) among its employees, it cannot allocate those restrictions in an unjust manner, for example, only to lower level employees. Subsequently, any such restrictions would have to be carefully justified, under Rawls's principles of justice.

Being fair and just with your employees would be the basis of Rawlsian philosophy in the workplace. If you want to treat your employees fairly, place yourself behind the *veil of ignorance*. With all other things being equal, if you would not want to be in their position from behind the *veil of ignorance*, then you are not treating them in a just manner.

Case Commentary: Aristotle and the Ethics of Virtue ————

Virtue ethics scrutinizes the character of the persons involved in a situation. We evaluate the morality of people's character as well as their actions. Of Aristotle's four cardinal virtues (courage, temperance, justice, and prudence or wisdom), one is especially relevant here: justice. If we pay an employee a just rate, he or she will receive exactly what they deserve. The salary will be based on job merit and requirements. Based on virtue ethics, we would never pay an employee according to how little we could get away with.

It is critical for managers to understand how employees view them, and their influence on decisions. It is also vital that managers understand that if they promote honest communication, they will create a comfortable environment, fostering honesty in the workplace.

Case Study—Discriminating Forces ————————————

Lenore Beck is the president of LB Consultants, Inc., located in Miami Beach, Florida. The company specializes in all aspects of the hospitality industry: food and beverage management, housekeeping, event management, and more. The company does most of its consulting in southeast Florida. However, in the last several years, the company has gained an excellent reputation in the Caribbean.

Lenore established her company ten years ago after she retired as regional director of human resource management for the Celebrity Hotel Group. Previous to that, she spent 22 years working at various hotel jobs, starting as a restaurant server in the hotel's main dining room while she was in college and graduating to a front desk position in her junior year. She was promoted to front desk manager three years later. Five years after that she became the assistant director of human resources, and eventually became the director of human resources. She held that position until she was promoted to the post of regional director.

Lenore is well known and well liked in the industry. She is acknowledged as fair, impartial, and considerate. Eleven of the fifteen consultants Lenore employs have been working for her for more than seven years; two of her consultants have been with her since she created the firm.

Recently, Lenore was contacted about a consulting job for the Windbreaker Resort, located on the very small and exclusive island of Elura in the Caribbean. Jim Wiley, the assistant general manager of the resort spoke to her on behalf of the resort's food and beverage manager, Jack Mallory. Mr. Mallory employs Chef Ronald, an excellent chef, known throughout the Caribbean for his culinary skills. However, he has shown himself not to be executive chef material. While creative in the kitchen, his purchasing and supervisory skills leave a lot to be desired. He often orders too much food, causing a lot of waste; or, he does not order enough food, creating dissatisfied guests. The kitchen always seems either overstaffed or understaffed, leaving the employees either unproductive or overly stressed.

Mr. Mallory had endured the situation for almost nine months, hoping that Chef Ronald would improve—until the incident with the Browns. The Browns, who have been guests at the hotel on and off for ten years, ordered 90 filet mignon dinners for their 25th wedding anniversary party at the resort. On the day of the dinner, only two hours before the function, Chef Ronald realized that he had only 50 filet mignons. Even after a mad scramble, he was unable to obtain the other 40. He hoped to solve the problem by offering all guests a wide selection including: grilled salmon, shrimp Creole, shrimp scampi, chicken Kiev, lobster tails, broiled chicken, prime rib, or filet mignon. That night there still were not enough filet mignons and the Browns were furious. They had reserved the party six months in advance and had paid in full the week before.

This is when Mr. Mallory asked Mr. Wiley for assistance and Mr. Wiley suggested Lenore's consulting firm. "I know each and every one of her consultants and they do an excellent job," Wiley stated. Mr. Mallory agreed and that is how Mr. Wiley came to be sitting in Ms. Beck's office just one week after the "Brown fiasco."

Mr. Wiley told Lenore, "I am interested in finding a consultant who will be knowledgeable in all aspects of food and beverage management. We are especially in need in the areas of purchasing and supervision." Wiley then gave Ms. Beck a shortened version of the "Brown fiasco."

Lenore replied, "I have just the person for you, Dave Maverick. He was the executive chef at the downtown Harris Hotel for 10 years before he came on board with us. As you know, the Harris Hotel has one of the busiest dining rooms throughout the year. Maverick did an outstanding job and I know for a fact that the Harris Hotel was very sorry to lose him. He has been with me now for seven years. He does a fantastic job!"

Mr. Wiley sat quietly for a moment. He knew that Ms. Beck was right; Maverick would do an excellent job. But he was hesitant anyway.

"This is between you and me Lenore. I can't have Maverick. Elura is a very backwards island and there is no respect for black men there. The chef would never even agree to work with Maverick."

Lenore was furious. She argued a bit with Wiley, but he would not budge. Finally, she agreed to send Jordan Hopkins, a blond haired, blue-eyed man whose family probably came over on the Mayflower. But she was angry. And mostly, she was angry with herself.

Case Questions

1. What are the ethical issues? Explain your answer.

2. What should Lenore do? Explain your answer.

3. Should cultural factors influence an ethical decision? Explain your answer based on the theories we have been studying.

Case Study—The Come On

Evan Berman is the human resources manager at the Athletics-to-Go Sports Arena located 30 miles south of Atlanta, Georgia. He has held the position for four years. For the previous six years, he was the human resources director for a large event management firm in Hoboken, New Jersey.

The arena employs over 500 people and is open 364 days a year. Evan has worked very hard at getting to know all of the employees. He enjoys walking through the arena at various times of the day to say hello and to stop for a chat. He is personally involved in all training sessions for new employees, which usually last from three days to two weeks, depending on the new positions being trained.

Jamie Lee is a new employee in the Athletics-to-Go Sports Arena box office. She is a recent college graduate and majored in sports management. This is her first post-college position. The only other job she had was waiting tables at the local college hangout. She sees the position in the arena box office as an opening into a career that she has always dreamed about. She aspires to a corporate level post, but she knows it will take much hard work and, probably, a graduate degree. That is another reason why she is so content with her job at the Athletics-to-Go Sports Arena. After one full year of employment, the company pays for related schooling as an employee benefit.

Jamie will not complete her probationary period for another 45 days. This is causing her a great deal of consternation because she has a problem and feels she should speak with someone in human resources. She finally decided to tell Evan that the executive vice president, Mr. Bentley Wilder, has been making suggestive comments to her and has been touching her inappropriately, causing her to feel very uncomfortable.

Obviously embarrassed, Jamie repeated some of the graphic language Wilder had used, including a tasteless, dirty joke that she had heard him tell at least three times in mixed company. Jamie told Evan that she politely asked Mr. Wilder to stop both the comments and the physical contact, but he just laughed it off and walked away. The unwanted behavior had been going on for three weeks. She didn't speak to Evan before because she did not want to come across as being overly sensitive. She added that she really enjoyed the job and was hoping to continue.

Evan asked Jamie if she would give him the afternoon to investigate the situation. Evan was a great deal more upset than he let on. For starters, Mr. Wilder is Evan's direct supervisor. Also, two other young women had approached Evan recently about Wilder's behavior. Evan had witnessed Wilder making inappropriate gestures and comments on many occasions. It seemed to Evan that Wilder thought he could do whatever he wanted. What was going to stop him? His family was the major shareholder in the publicly held Athletics-to-Go Sports Arena.

Case Questions

1. What are the ethical issues involved?

2. What should Evan do? Explain your answer

3. Did Jamie do the right thing by going to Evan with her complaint? Explain your answer.

4. Should Jamie have waited until she finished her probationary period? Explain your answer.

Case Study—Is this Sexual Harassment?

Carl Bloom had been the assistant manager at the Pearson Hotel for three years. He is 60 years old and has been connected to the hotel industry for most of his adult life. He has held many jobs over the years, including high-level administrative positions.

This summer, the Pearson Hotel hosted fifteen college interns from Northcoast University. The interns worked for six weeks, each week doing a different job. It was Carl's job to oversee the organization of the intern schedule. It was also his responsibility to collect evaluations from the interns' supervisors and administer grades for Northcoast University. He had complete oversight for the grading process.

The interns had weekends free and were allowed to travel. Carl had become particularly friendly with one of the interns, Christopher Blake. Christopher was a bit older than the rest of the interns. He had turned 35 during their stay at the Pearson. The difference in the maturity level between Christopher and the rest of the students was obvious. Carl sought Christopher's company on a regular basis.

Even though hotel regulations stated that there was to be no fraternizing between interns and hotel staff, Carl asked Christopher to join him in Carson City for a concert. He told Christopher that he had tickets for a JB Lincoln concert, a very popular local rock group, and that they could share a hotel room.

Both Carl and Christopher were aware of the strict hotel regulations. Carl told Christopher that nobody needed to know. If anybody asked, Carl would say that he was going to Carson City with a friend and Christopher could say he was going to Gemstone, a town 30 miles south of Carson City, to visit relatives.

Carl mentioned his plans to his co-worker Alice, the dining room manager. Alice became upset. She was angry with Carl for putting her in the situation of knowing that he was breaking the company's rules. She was also concerned because she was quite aware that Carl and Christopher were of the same sexual orientation. Carl told her there was nothing to worry about.

Alice stewed about the situation overnight. She finally decided to bring it to the attention of Margaret, her supervisor. When she spoke with Margaret, she also shared some of Carl's history that she was sure Margaret was unaware of. Alice told Margaret that Carl had once been her boss and that Carl was asked to leave his position because he was sexually harassing one of the busboys. The employee brought a suit against the hotel and the hotel asked Carl to leave quietly, promising that the matter would not be made public.

Shortly thereafter, Alice had bumped into Carl at an educator's meeting where she had been asked to speak about hotel internships. Carl had become a teacher of hotel management in one of the local high schools. A few months later,

Alice had read an article about Carl in the newspaper stating that two male students brought a harassment charge against Carl, but that the charges were dropped. Carl "resigned" his position shortly afterwards. A few months later, Carl secured the position with Pearson and had been there ever since.

Margaret was flabbergasted. She immediately called Jane Hunt, director of human resources for the Pearson. Jane was out of town but she told Margaret to wait out the situation, promising that she would speak with Carl after the weekend.

Margaret was stunned. She wondered how the company would feel if she went off for a weekend with a male student, sharing a hotel room. She felt that Carl was abusing his power as a supervisor. Margaret did not know if the student felt pressured to go because, in addition to everything else, Carl was to administer the student's grade, which was for a full semester's worth of credit. She just didn't know what to do.

Case Questions

1. What are the ethical issues involved here? Explain your answer.

2. Considering the fact that Mr. Bloom is to grade Christopher on his work, is it ethical for them to spend social time together? Explain your answer.

3. Did Jane Hunt act in an ethical manner? Explain your answer.

4. What would you have done if you were Margaret? Explain your answer.

Case Study—Taking Credit

Kaye Goodman is the restaurant manager of Fortune Eatery in Hollywood, Florida. Kaye has been in the restaurant industry for more than 30 years. She has worked in managerial positions for several large chain operations around the country. She was recruited five years ago to take over the Hollywood restaurant because it was underperforming in a very competitive market. Since she arrived, sales at the restaurant increased significantly each year and turnover was next to zero. Whenever Fortune Eatery's national director, Dudley Cash, visited he was astonished at the difference not only in the revenue, but in the restaurant's ambiance as well. The atmosphere was cordial and the staff was always friendly and helpful. Kaye wanted to add regional food items to the menu for quite some time. Although she was promised a certain amount of autonomy when she accepted the job, Kaye found it very difficult to maneuver through Fortune Eatery's bureaucracy.

Fortune Eatery is a national restaurant chain with 250 units across the country. Corporate offices are located in Denver, Colorado. Purchasing is centralized at the Denver offices and coordinated through purchasing directors in each state. The chain has regional as well as state operations directors who support the units in their areas.

Lorna Chandler is Fortune Eatery's operations director for the state of Florida. Lorna is a young, ambitious woman who wants to climb the corporate ladder of Fortune Eatery. While in college, she worked part time at corporate headquarters and at their flagship restaurant in Denver. Later, she opened the company's first restaurant in Florida and eventually became the operations director for all ten units in the state. Lorna works closely with Dolly Crassly, Fortune Eatery's director of purchasing for the Florida units. Their offices are located in a building adjacent to the restaurant managed by Kaye Goodman.

Kaye and her assistant manager, Stan Hensley, took the initiative to conduct a very thorough marketing study on what they refer to as menu item #99—a Caribbean barbeque sandwich accompanied by a specially formulated jicama slaw. This was in keeping with Kaye's desire to introduce regional foods at her restaurant. Their marketing study and other paperwork went back and forth between corporate and the restaurant until finally Kay was told by the national sales director, Barbie Droop, to hold off on the item for at least a year because they wanted to try it in Denver first. Kaye tried to explain to Ms. Droop that the sandwich probably would not be successful in Denver; the target was the Florida market. However, Ms. Droop made it abundantly clear to Kaye that corporate would handle the matter.

Six months later, there was no progress with menu item #99. The Denver office was not doing a thing. Kaye went to Lorna and explained that she was worried another Florida restaurant would soon offer something similar. Lorna admired Kaye's entrepreneurial spirit and respected her savvy in regard to culinary and marketing issues. Lorna suggested that they talk with Dan Mason, Fortune Eatery's regional director of operations. Mr. Mason was due to visit the Florida office the next day.

After Mr. Mason heard from both Kaye and Lorna, he felt sure that they had to move on the item as soon as possible. He suggested that they roll it out the next quarter—but keep everything quiet in the meantime. Mr. Mason finished the meeting by stating, "This region knows what this region wants; the heck with them at corporate!" Kaye was excited and began putting everything in motion.

Three weeks before the scheduled rollout, Kaye left for a conference on food service management in Philadelphia. While she was gone, Doris Yenterley, Fortune Eatery's corporate vice president of purchasing called Dolly Crassly, the Florida director of purchasing and asked, "What's going on Dolly? Why are you ordering all these weird spices? I've never even heard of some of them." Dolly had no idea what Doris was talking about, but she told her she would get to the bottom of it immediately.

When she hung up Dolly went across to Lorna's office and asked her about the strange purchases. Lorna shrugged her shoulders and said, "I haven't a clue. Kaye's out of town but let's call her assistant manager, Stan." Lorna put Stan on the speakerphone so Dolly could hear. Stan started to explain, "It's for the new menu item, menu item #99." He started to say something directly to Lorna, but she cut him off. Lorna told Dolly that she knew "absolutely nothing" about menu item #99.

When Kaye returned from the conference she found a complete upheaval regarding menu item #99. She tried explaining to Dolly and others that she was told to keep quiet about the development and the rollout, but no one believed her. She went to see Lorna who replied, "If anyone ever asks me if I had previous knowledge of what you intended to do, I will emphatically tell them that I didn't know a thing."

Kaye was stupefied. She had no choice but to continue on with her plans to roll out the new menu item. The corporate office took over the glamour of "opening day" festivities, while Kaye and Stan were left with the grunt work. When the day came it was a great success. Menu item #99 was very well received. The next day, the local section of the newspaper had a front page story. The headline read, "The Fortune Eatery Corporation does it again!" The picture below the article showed Lorna Chandler in the front center postion, flanked on one side by Dan Mason, Dudley Cash, and Doris Yenterley and on the other side by Barbie Droop and Dolly Crassly.

Case Questions

1. What are the ethical issues? Explain your answer.

2. Was Kaye treated in an ethical manner? Explain your answer.

3. What would you do if you were Kaye? Explain your answer.

4. What would you have done if you were Lorna? Explain your answer.

5. Apply each of the ethical theories we have studied to this case. Explain each of your applications.

Case Study—Stars Are Difficult to Come By

As the food and beverage director of a 400-room hotel on Atlantic Beach in North Carolina, Mr. Mason knew the value of a star employee. Jenny, his "star" waitress, worked for the hotel for the last four years. She started in the pantry and then became a line cook. When she became pregnant, management moved her to the front of the house where she worked as a hostess.

After she had her baby, she returned as a waitress, and loved it. The flexible schedule was important to her and she appreciated the extra tip money. The guests were very fond of her and frequently requested her services. Management thought highly of her; she was excellent in "up-selling" and she was truly a "Jack of all trades." In an emergency, she could fill in for almost any position in the restaurant, kitchen, or banquets. She was even capable of managing the restaurant when necessary.

Mr. Mason had recently asked Jenny to become an assistant manager. The hotel's general manager, Mr. Roberts, discouraged the promotion. He reminded Mr. Mason that Jenny already had one written and two verbal warnings for tardiness and absenteeism. Nonetheless, he allowed Mr. Mason to go ahead and make the offer. Jenny turned down the assistant manager position. She did not want to take on the additional responsibility and was not ready to give up the money she made as a waitress.

A few weeks later, on a busy Friday afternoon, Jenny called in at 3 P.M. (her shift started at 4 P.M.), saying that she didn't have a babysitter and couldn't come to work. That same night, Mr. Roberts saw her at a local concert with her friends.

On Monday morning, a written suspension and discharge notice for Jenny was on Mr. Mason's desk ready for his signature. Mr. Mason called Mr. Roberts and convinced him to give the "star," Jenny, another chance. He pleaded his case by stressing how difficult it was to find someone as versatile and well liked as Jenny. However, Mr. Mason also understood that he was skirting his own ethical creed. Other associates were fired for lesser infractions. Later that day, Mr. Mason had a long talk with Jenny and made her understand this was her last chance.

Case Questions

1. How would a rule utilitarian look at this situation? Explain your answer.

2. How would John Rawls's approach this situation? Explain your answer.

3. What would you have done if you were Mr. Mason? Why?

This case was authored by Jude Ferreira, Assistant Professor of Hospitality Management, Johnson & Wales University, Florida Campus.

Case Study—Blue Vest Pizza and Customer Satisfaction

At the Corporate Office

"The logic is simple," said Tom, the new director of guest service relations for Blue Vest Pizza, Inc. "If we increase our customer satisfaction we will increase sales. More customers are going to visit our restaurants because of our quality service. And if we increase sales, we will increase profits."

"But how can our restaurants demonstrate that they have increased customer service?" asked Lori, the company's skeptical but loyal director of operations.

"We embark on a full-blown measurement initiative," Tom replied. "I'm proposing a three-pronged approach. First, we fully stock our restaurants with comment cards. We make sure that every server presents a card and pen to each table at the same time the check is presented. It will also be the responsibility of each server to collect his or her comment cards and turn them into the store management.

"Second, because each store has the name and phone number of our take-out and delivery customers, we can access that database to contact a sample of each store's customers. We can hire an outside marketing service and have it call twenty customers per store who have recently dined there. We can ask questions pertaining to the speed and quality of service, the quality of the food, and whether or not they plan on returning to their local Blue Vest Pizza within the next two to three weeks. From that data we can draw correlations between our service quality and customer loyalty.

"And finally, and perhaps most important," Tom continued, "We can base our managers' quarterly bonuses on their customer service levels. Managers who can provide exceptional quality service and build customer loyalty will receive the bigger bonuses. Managers who fail to do so will receive little or no bonus."

"That's brilliant!" said Joe, the CEO for Blue Vest Pizza. "Now all our managers will want to work hard to ensure good customer service. Their bonuses will depend on it."

"Correct," said Tom. "And, both sales and profits will be increasing at the same time. It cannot miss."

"Hmm… I'm not too sure of this," said Lori. "I'll approve the initiative, but I'm going to be very surprised if it works."

At a Local Blue Vest Pizza

"This new customer service initiative sucks," complained Hal, the manager of the Berkley Ville Blue Vest Pizza. "Does the corporate office even know what goes on in their restaurants? How can I concentrate on all phases of my business if I'm in a constant worry about giving one customer bad service? Besides, I have a very high volume store. I can't always guarantee that every single customer is going to receive the best service. Even worse, I might lose my bonus. I was counting on that money to pay for my vacation this year."

"I'm with you," said Sarah, the Blue Vest Pizza manager in East Salamone, who was on the other end of the telephone. "But I've been studying the initiative closely. I think there's a way we can all get around it."

"How is that possible?" Hal asked.

"Look at the distribution and collection procedures for the comment cards. Do you think that servers in their right minds would want to hand a comment card to a table they just had a problem with?"

"Of course not," Hal said.

"Then why give one to them?" Sarah said in a sneaky yet playful voice. "We can shred the bad comment cards. Or, we can just fill out the cards ourselves, making them up so they have nothing but glowing things to say. We would certainly want to put in a bad card from time to time, just to show that we're not perfect. But for the most part, we can go through all the cards and make sure 99 percent of them are good."

"It's unethical," Hal said. "Besides, how can we get past this new initiative where our customers are called at random?"

"We have to remember that they will only call the people whose phone numbers are in our store database. We can get into our database from time to time and change some of the phone numbers. For example, instead of leaving in the customer's number, we can switch it out with the phone numbers of our friends. That way there's a better chance that they will call people who will cover for us."

"That sure is sneaky," said Hal, "but it will be fun switching out some of the numbers. I know a lot of people who would be willing to help me out."

"Something else we can do," continued Sarah, "is not answer the phone when we are really busy. The way I see it, if I can't guarantee the customer good service, why bother to go after their business?"

"That happens to me all the time," Hal said. "Since my restaurant is so busy, the phone rings like crazy on Friday and Saturday nights. I'll have my regular restaurant customers to take care of. They are my first priority. Besides, most nights one of my employees always calls in sick or doesn't show up. When I'm a person or two short, this carryout and delivery business is just a nuisance. Since my bonus will no longer be based on sales, it really doesn't matter to me whether they buy from my restaurant or my competitors!"

"Absolutely," said Sarah. "With the new system in place, we're all better off concentrating on our dine-in customers anyway. Taking the phones off the hook on a busy night from time to time is the realistic thing to do."

"Thanks, Sarah. I feel much better now. As far as I'm concerned, my bonus is the most important part of my job. If I ever stopped receiving one, I would look for another job. It's as simple as that."

At the Corporate Office—One Year Later

"I simply do not understand this," a surprised Joe, the CEO for Blue Vest Pizza, began. "Our records show that our customer satisfaction and loyalty levels are at an all time high, yet this has been our worst year for sales growth. How do you account for this Tom?"

"I'm just as much in the dark as you are about this sir," the embarrassed director of guest service relations replied. "This has all been very confusing and counter to the logic behind customer service fundamentals. Some of our restaurants with the highest customer satisfaction levels are showing negative sales growth, while some restaurants with high sales growth actually have poor customer service ratings. How can this be?"

"Our system of implementation and accountability was all wrong," said Lori, the director of operations. "The majority of our managers are good people and want to do the right thing, but we created a system that pitted their ideals and ethics against their checkbooks. We were bound to fail. It's time to re-examine the initiative."

Case Questions:

1. How was the customer service evaluation system implemented by Blue Vest Pizza flawed? Explain your answer through the lens of either a utilitarian or a Kantian thinker.

2. How can a corporation ensure the ethical nature of a customer service evaluation system, such as the one being implemented at Blue Vest Pizza? Explain your answer.

3. If you were a manager in this company, what would you have done?

4. Do you believe that these types of situations are common or uncommon in the restaurant industry? Why do you feel that way?

This case was authored by Alan Seidman, DBA, Associate Professor of Hospitality Management, Johnson & Wales University, Florida Campus.

Case Study—But Can She Do the Job?

Michele Danforth had been a part of the hotel industry her entire life. She grew up in a hotel owned jointly by her parents and grandparents and worked in the family hotel all through high school. When she went to college, she worked over twenty hours a week at various hotels near the school.

After Michele received her bachelor's degree in hospitality management, she decided that she wanted to work in New York City. She had several decent offers at graduation and accepted a management trainee position at the Belle Grande on New York City's trendy upper east side. She chose to go with the Belle Grande chain for several reasons. The most important reason was because it was a small, but rapidly growing chain. She thought she would make it into the corporate level much sooner than she would with other hotel companies.

Two years later, Michele applied for a corporate level position. She felt she was ready and she had excellent reviews from her supervisors. However, she was passed over and the job was given to a young man who had graduated in the class after hers at the same university where she had studied.

Michele was mystified. She spoke with Margaret in the human resources office. Michele asked her how many women worked at the corporate level. Margaret told her she was not allowed to give out that information.

Case Questions

1. Are there any ethical issues involved? If so, what are they? Explain your answer.

2. Is Margaret treating Jane in an unethical manner? Or is she just doing her job? Explain your answer.

11

Applying Ethics to Maintain an Environmentally Sound Hospitality and Tourism Industry

Eᴀᴄʜ ʏᴇᴀʀ ᴍᴏʀᴇ ᴛʜᴀɴ 150 million tons of pollutants are pumped into the air we breathe, more than 41 million tons of toxic wastes are produced, and 15 million gallons of pollutants are dumped into the nation's waterways.[1] The total United States energy consumption each year is equivalent to about 2,134,960,000 tons of oil.[2] On average, each American citizen produces over 4 pounds of garbage every day.

The hospitality and tourism industry does not exist in a vacuum. There are very specific environmental areas that relate to this industry: water pollution, noise pollution, deforestation, depletion of species and habitats, solid waste management, recycling, and others. The entire hospitality and tourism industry depends on one form or another of the natural environment for the energy it uses, the material resources it needs, and for waste disposal. The environment, in turn, is affected by the industry's commercial activities.

Guestrooms can produce large amounts of waste, ranging from one-half pound to 28 pounds per day, depending on the number of occupants and the type of property. Aluminum cans, bottles, newspapers, and magazines—typical guestroom refuse—are all recyclable. Other waste materials produced by a lodging facility include cardboard boxes, cooking oil, and office paper. Additionally, any type of construction project can produce yard waste and debris from demolition.[3] Waste of water occurs when a facility launders linens and towels that have barely been used.

---

[1] Manuel G. Velasquez, Business Ethics: Concepts and Cases, 5th ed. (Upper Saddle River, N.J.: Prentice Hall, 2002), p. 206.

[2] Lester Brown, "Challenges of the New Century," in State of the World 2000 (New York: WW Norton & Company, 2000), pp. 5–8.

[3] Rhonda Sherman, "Waste Reduction and Recycling for the Lodging Industry," North Carolina Cooperative Extension Service, AG-473-17 WQWM-128.

Companies are citizens in their communities. Hospitality and tourism businesses can exert influence on their communities, including in the environmental arena. Managers, employees, shareholders, guests, and the community are all environmental actors—whether they understand their roles or not. Businesses have a responsibility to conduct their affairs in a manner that sustains the environment upon which we all depend.

Below is a case involving a cruise line. A ship is a citizen within many different communities: its ports of call, its main harbor, and the waters in which it travels. A cruise ship can bring riches as well as misfortune to any place it sails. As you read the case, imagine yourself a crewmember on this ship and decide what you would do in this situation.

🔍 Case Study—Gray Water/Black Water Overflow

Super Cruise Line Inc. owns five large cruise ships operating from Gulf of Mexico ports in the southern United States. The ships offer seven-day round trip voyages to Cozumel, Belize, and the Cayman Islands, entertaining guests with world class performers, warm sunshine, plentiful food and drink, and activities ranging from the mundane "sit by the pool exercise" to the exploration of the ancient Mayan ruins of the Yucatan Peninsula. Ships operate as floating cities—comparable in terms of complexity to a utility and public works department of a small shore-side community. Concurrent with the principal focus of entertaining guests, ships must operate in a safe and environmentally responsible manner, complying with the regulations of international maritime law, various federal laws, and the local regulations of the ports they visit. Compliance to law is mandated by the company's environmental management policies and procedures.

Two of the dominant waste streams are black water and gray water. Black water is the term used for the waste stream generated by the ship from toilets, urinals, and drainage from the ship's infirmaries (including wash basins and wash tubs) located in the medical area. Gray water is the waste stream generated by the ship, for example, effluent from galley services (such as sinks, drains, dishwashers, etc.), laundry services, showers, baths, and washbasin drains. If gray water becomes mixed with black water, the entire mixture would then be classified as black water, which is regulated more strictly than gray water.

All persons, passengers, and crew members aboard a ship add to the two waste streams. Due to the nature of a ship's construction and the inability to hold this water for longer than 48–76 hours because of limited tank space, the waste requires continual management by ship officers. Black water is always treated to an acceptable level through a United States Coast Guard–approved Marine Sanitation Device

(MSD) before being discharged overboard. At Super Cruise Line Inc., gray water waste is held while in port and then discharged untreated into the sea. The company allows discharge of these wastes only outside of twelve nautical miles from land and marine sanctuaries, even though discharge is usually allowed by most port regulations while in port. In fact, most commercial ships routinely discharge in port.

While all waste is processed according to international law and the laws of the States in which ships visit, the Company has instituted a policy that exceeds regulatory compliance requirements. It believes that protecting the marine environment protects the beautiful destinations in which its ships operate and its guests enjoy. It makes good business sense to preserve the environment.

In some areas, such as the State of Florida, Super Cruise Line Inc. entered into a voluntary, formal agreement with State regulators, agreeing not to discharge either gray or black water into any Florida waters.

However, one Saturday afternoon in December, in the Port of Tampa, there was an accidental release of both gray water and black water. The situation surrounding the release began as a typical busy turnaround day in port with disembarking guests passing through Customs and Immigration en route to their transportation home. At the same time, new guests were preparing to board for the next cruise. The ship's officers and crew were putting the ship in order for the next voyage. The hotel staff was washing linens and cleaning over a thousand cabins as the engineering staff loaded fuels and supplies for the coming voyage.

Edward Smythe, a young man of 29 years of age, was in charge of the engineering watch. He was a European but licensed as an engineer by the country of Liberia. His responsibilities included the operation of the engineering plant and the management of his assistants. Although young, he was an experienced engineer. However, his experience was mostly gained aboard commercial tank ships transporting gasoline between South Africa and Europe. This was his second voyage aboard a cruise ship and his first as the responsible person for the engineering plant. His immediate supervisor was the chief engineer, Dominick Dupree. The Chief, as he is called, was responsible for the entire engineering department of the ship. He managed a staff of 75 operators and maintenance personnel.

The Chief was 55 years old and well experienced aboard cruise ships. He had operated cruise ships for 30 years and had been employed by Super Cruise Line Inc. for the past 19 years, the last 5 years as chief engineer.

The Chief was second in command seven years ago when he witnessed an incident that would later result in a $7 million fine and *seven years of probation for the company because the previous chief engineer was found to have illegally dumped water mixed with oil into the sea for over two years. The previous Chief's attitude was very cavalier, saying the ocean could "take it" and the machinery was more trouble to run than it was worth. Because of this criminal activity, he spent a year in prison.*

Consequently, the current chief engineer had first-hand knowledge about the fact that it was not worth "cutting corners" when it came to obeying the law. Through the seven-year probationary period he and his colleagues learned to go beyond compliance. This attitude was deeply instilled in him as the company went through a cultural change resulting in a real appreciation for the environment, followed by a mandate to protect it as best they could. Chief Dupree became committed; he promised never to allow himself or his staff to take shortcuts regarding the environmental aspects of the operation aboard his ship. This culture was the one that the new engineer, Edward Smythe, found himself in; it contrasted sharply from the culture in which he was trained. That culture was one of cutting corners whenever possible in order to increase profits.

About 1:00 P.M. on that turnaround day, Edward Smythe was a busy man. He was responsible for loading fuel and potable water into the tanks of the ship. His staff was performing maintenance, and the hotel staff was busy cleaning the ship. During this period, large volumes of water were being sent to the holding tanks. This included black water from the toilets, gray water from the showers, laundry water from the washers, and water from the floors being scrubbed. Additionally, the galleys had generated large volumes of water from cooking and cleaning after the breakfast meal for 3,500 people. When cooking for lunch began, the waste water load was already abnormally high.

Furthermore, during the previous week's cruise, the ship experienced a failure of the black water treatment equipment. Because of this, Chief Dupree ordered the holding of all black water for the three days that it would take to reactivate the system. Chief Dupree planned to hold the waste until the treatment system was repaired and then treat what was held before discharging any of it into the sea.

Unfortunately, the generation of the week's black water was twenty percent over the normal production. Although the Chief calculated that he had sufficient holding capacity until the system was fixed and the effluent could be processed overboard on Sunday, he did not anticipate the extra load from the additional cleaning during the turnaround day, Saturday.

Smythe, fully aware of Chief Dupree's plan, became alarmed when he saw that, of the three tanks holding the excess black water, two were completely full and the third was rising quickly, soon to reach its maximum capacity. There were no extra tanks to put the rising black water into, except for one gray water tank. Despite the fact that it was acceptable to use the gray water tank for this purpose, it was not normally done aboard company ships.

Smythe decided to open the proper valves, start the pump and transfer half of the almost full black water tank to the gray water tank. This put both tanks at half capacity. During the operation he became distracted when the electrical generator, a critical piece of machinery, indicated a malfunction in its cooling circuit. He changed focus and became involved with addressing the problem with the cooling circuit on the generator. He stopped the pump transferring black water to the gray water tanks, but he forgot to close the valves. For the next three hours the open valves allowed water to flow freely into the tanks.

At 4:00 P.M., the bridge officer, Mr. Jamison, noticed some liquid spilling out of the vent on the port side of the ship. He called the engine control room and informed Smythe of the leakage. Smythe told Mr. Jamison that there was no pumping operation going on at the moment and not to "bother him," as he was busy with other tasks. But the bridge officer Jamison, having worked through the same environmental cultural transformation as Chief Dupree, immediately called the captain and chief engineer. Chief Dupree went straight away to the engine space to investigate and discovered the open valves. He closed the valves without delay, and the flow overboard stopped. The time it took from the first sighting of the leakage to the cessation of the overflow was about 15 minutes.

Chief Dupree then proceeded to the engine control room. Upon entering he confronted Smythe who uttered, "It's not my fault." But Chief Dupree was less concerned with "fault" than with ensuring that proper immediate actions were taken. He tried to help Smythe understand that "transparency" is the key word in all environmental operations. Nevertheless, Smythe kept insisting that he was not at fault.

Before long, the Chief had enough information from the ship's machinery automation systems to understand what had transpired. He was able to identify when the valves had been opened and the times that the pumps were started and stopped. He also established that Smythe neglected to close the valves and that the overflow of the gray water tank into the sea resulted from gravity flow of the waste waters into the tanks from above. After he completed his investigation, the Chief left the control room to discuss the event with the captain.

Dupree briefed both the captain and the environmental officer. Every ship has an environmental officer to oversee environmental compliance; he reports directly to the captain. Afterwards, the three contacted the shore-side environmental compliance department to report the violation via speaker telephone. The time was 4:30 P.M. It took thirty minutes from the time of the overflow sighting to the first report.

These officers were aware of the culture that existed prior to the Environmental Compliance Plan and the probation days in the company's history. They knew that this type of reporting would never have happened so quickly then, if at all. Subsequent to a short discussion, everyone mobilized to report the events to the United States Coast Guard and the State environmental authorities.

First, they contacted the local United States Coast Guard Marine Safety Office and reported that approximately three cubic meters of gray water, mixed with untreated black water, had overflowed into the sea, and therefore the spillage was illegal. Secondly, they contacted the Florida authorities. All the details were fully and completely revealed to the authorities within sixty minutes of the event.

An investigation team was dispatched from the company's environmental management department. The team was scheduled to arrive at the next port of call which was Cozumel, Mexico.

This case was authored by Robert C. Spicer, Environmental Compliance Officer, Carnival Cruise Lines and Roberta Schwartz, Instructor, Johnson & Wales University, Florida Campus.

Case Commentary: The Company

A utilitarian, a Kantian, and a justice ethicist would all give the company a positive ethical review. After committing some serious errors in the past, the company turned itself around and created a corporate culture that includes putting a very high value on protecting the environment. Moreover, it has backed this corporate culture with training.

From a utilitarian perspective, all of the company's recent actions are to be praised. The company is clearly promoting "the greatest good for the greatest number" by taking critical action to ensure that the environment is protected. In addition, it has taken its environmental obligations seriously enough to instill strict corporate practices and to train its personnel to adhere strictly to those practices. All of this demonstrates ethical behavior from both an act utilitarian and a rule utilitarian perspective.

Kant would be concerned with the company's true motivation. Are the new practices and new corporate culture really a change of heart from previous negligent behavior? Are they indeed evidence of a new ethical perspective based on responsibility to others? Assuming that the new attitude is a genuine change of heart, Kant would laud the company for its strong adherence to an ethic of duty to others through its environmental practices. The rights of others are being respected by this company, which is not attempting to hide facts from others, or to deceive them.

Likewise, both justice ethics and virtue ethics would praise the actions and the character of this company and its leadership. Justice is being served by ensuring that environmental pollution (an "externality" to the company's profit and loss statement if the company can get away with polluting while the taxpaying public picks up the tab) does not unjustly harm those least advantaged. Additionally, those corporate officers formulating and carrying out the company's strong environmental protection policies display strong, virtuous character.

Despite all of its good intentions, the company has inadvertently committed another environmental infraction. Should the company be held responsible for the action of one of its employees, even if that employee had been trained regarding the protection of the environment?

There are two justice questions at play here: compensation and retribution. First let's look at compensation. The company should unquestionably pay for any necessary clean up. The company may also incur some further expenses, perhaps to retrain Smythe or to train additional diligent new personnel working in this area, but beyond that no other compensatory costs are evident in this case.

Beyond compensation, is retribution warranted in this case? Should it be heavily fined for this violation? This company should not be fined because it has diligently attempted to work within the law and has shown itself to be reasonably responsible. In this particular instance, it is clear that they jumped into action to curtail the situation as quickly as possible as soon as they discovered the error, and that they promptly and honestly reported the matter to authorities.

Beyond a fine, retribution could also involve some other category of penalty for the company. Examples might include an additional probationary period or other curtailments of its activities. But, again, there appears to be little basis for retribution in this case. The company acted responsibly and promptly when it learned of the leakage. It had worked very hard at training employees and endeavored to maintain an environmentally sensitive corporate culture. In fact, in this case, the worst that could possibly be said against the company is that it hired the wrong employee, Smythe. At most, any reprisal should be minor. For instance, the company might be told that the violation will be marked onto its record, or it might receive a written warning about the spillage.

Case Commentary: The Individuals

Chief Dupree, bridge officer Jamison, the environmental officer and the captain are all to be commended for their swift and timely action. If they had not moved so quickly, the spill could have been much worse. They had been through similar circumstances; they put training and knowledge into action, and brought a potential disaster under control.

There is still the question of Mr. Smythe, the engineer who became distracted, thereby allowing the spillage to occur in the first place. The same two justice questions that we discussed earlier are at play again: the issues of compensation and retribution. First let's look at retribution. Should Mr. Smythe be punished for allowing the spillage to occur? And if so, how severe should the punishment be?

Mr. Smythe should definitely face some type of retribution. He failed to close the proper valves; he allowed himself to become distracted in a key situation, which showed him to be unreliable; and he was dismissive to a crewmember when the crewmember tried to bring significant information to his attention. The ethical question becomes whether or not his carelessness was reckless and morally wrong. However, no great, lasting harm transpired, and the carelessness may be understandable, so one might not think that Smythe's behavior was unethical. Therefore, perhaps no major ethical question concerning Smythe is involved. A spillage occurred that could be cleaned up.

On the other hand, Smythe also was unwilling to accept the responsibility for his actions. He immediately claimed that the action was not his fault. Furthermore, he was unable to understand that fault was not the issue at hand; the danger to the environment was the fundamental matter.

Assuming that Smythe has engaged in morally problematic behavior, what is the wisest course of action by the company toward this employee? Possible courses of action range all the way from severe punishment, such as discharge, to taking no action at all. Probably neither course of action is wise or warranted. A middle course, such as additional training and milder punishment (probation, suspension, etc.) may be the wisest course of action to follow.

If we were to examine the overall situation strictly from a utilitarian perspective, we could measure the benefit against the harm. How much harm is going to occur from the spill? Will marine life be devastated for years? Or, will the spill dissolve quickly and not have any lasting effect? If it is the latter, actual harms are not that many. A utilitarian would also focus on the actions taken to avoid errors such as the spillage. For example, the company has trained its employees. This has enabled the company to support the environment in all of the communities it serves, even when mishaps like this occur.

A utilitarian might also scrutinize the legalities of the situation. The cruise line has shown itself to be a good business recently because it has avoided getting into serious trouble; it has done everything possible to avoid lawsuits and bad publicity. The predominant view here might be that good ethics is good for business.

Finally, we might ask if firing Smythe would lead to better consequences for everyone involved. A utilitarian would say that he should not be let off the hook completely, because it could likely lead to other infractions, either by Smythe or others who see him "get off the hook." Some type of penalty is warranted, because that will lead to better long-term consequences. A rule utilitarian would insist on a universal way to treat all employees who commit environmental violations. However Smythe is to be treated for his infraction, is the way all employees should be treated for similar infractions.

As stated earlier, Kant would agree that the organization has done its part, although the ethical praise it deserves for this behavior would depend entirely on its intentions: is it "doing right" because it is *good for the environment* or because it is *good for business?* If the former, praise is merited; if the latter, the behavior has no particular moral significance.

Kant would find Smythe's behavior to be ethically problematic. Smythe was not following the categorical imperative when he failed to treat others and their welfare as paramount (as an "end in itself"), and his refusal to take responsibility for his own actions shows a further unwillingness to do his duty to other humans. He has shown himself to be morally irresponsible.

From a justice perspective, Rawls would find polluting our environment to be unjust to the many who depend, indirectly or directly, on that part of our environment. A brief step behind the *veil of ignorance* quickly reveals this. So, Smythe's actions have also led to an injustice, albeit a relatively minor one since the problem was discovered and corrected so quickly. The remaining justice question is what form of retribution Smythe should face, a matter discussed earlier.

Aristotle examines a person's character. He would find both Chief Dupree and bridge officer Jamison to be of fine moral character. They both showed courage and prudence (wisdom) through their immediate actions. Conversely, Smythe showed himself to be unethical for two reasons. First, he evaded his responsibility by claiming that the leakage was not his fault. This demonstrated a lack of both courage and honesty. Second, he exhibited a distinct lack of prudence through his careless behavior. According to Aristotle, Smythe did not act in a reasonable fashion. He failed to exercise reason and lacks character.

Case Study—All Roads Lead to the Resort

The Escape Now Resort Conglomerate (ENRC) has been searching for a new Resort and Spa location. The company has finally decided on a pristine beach on the island of Madreha in the Caribbean. Madreha is a small island, hardly known outside the immediate vicinity, with very high unemployment. The local government has been seeking a remedy to the work problem and has high hopes for the new resort.

The new resort will host 300 guestrooms, 2 Olympic sized swimming pools, and 6 lighted tennis courts. Golf will be offered at a local course two miles inland. At present, there is only one two-lane road that leads out to this area of the coastline because the only inhabitants are a small group of retirees. Other than that, the area is enclosed by natural forestation.

People First, a local activist group, has researched ENRC. People First claims that the ENRC has a history of not fulfilling its promises to the communities where they build. It wants the local government to set up a contract that delineates any consequences that will result if ENRC does not keep its word on all the promised measures.

People First called a meeting, which was attended by 250 people. This was a very large turnout for such a small island. The guest speaker was Ronald Avery, an engineer specializing in construction management. Mr. Avery stated that the basic infrastructure of Madreha would not support the type of resort that ENRC was proposing. New roads would have to be built. "Consider where these roads will be built," he emphasized. "And the sewage system is not appropriately set up for such a large structure," he continued. He further discussed noise issues, electricity, water, and a host of other topics the islanders had to consider.

"But, the jobs! We will all have jobs!" someone in the crowd shouted out.

People First representative, Claire Muller, called the meeting back to order. "We have to consider all sides of this equation. Maybe it is possible to have it all."

"But the island will suffer," another person stated. "It will become noisy and overrun with tourists and we'll all have $6 per hour jobs. That's not much better than we have now."

"At least we'll all have jobs," another islander said.

It went on and on. Finally, it was decided that the group would put together a community contract. A group from People First would speak with local government officials, insisting that ENRC sign the contract. Consequences would be clearly defined.

The group met with Archibald Sander, Assistant to the Governor. Their requests to ENRC included the following:

1. 80 percent of all construction jobs including construction management positions, would go to islanders.

2. 80 percent of all resort positions would go to islanders.

3. Jobs would pay, at a minimum, $7 per hour.

4. All sewage, water, and electrical systems would be appropriately updated in order to support 1,000 more people per day after the resort is completed.

5. Noise ordinances would be put into effect.

6. Two new roads into and out of the planned resort area would be built. The roads would each be two-lane roads in keeping with the area's present forestation. A minimal number of trees would be cut down. People First would be involved in the selection of the tree paths as well as the acceptance of the trees to be cut.

Archibald Sander agreed with all the provisions in the document. He brought the contract to the Governor, Landon Lamar. Mr. Lamar knew it would be difficult for ENRC to agree to all of the requests, but he said he would meet with them and see what he could do.

The following week both Mr. Sander and Mr. Lamar met with Rad Hopkins, director of construction for ENRC. Surprisingly, Mr. Hopkins agreed to most of the provisions. He said he would give 75 percent of jobs to the islanders and he would pay the $7 per hour job rate. He said he would meet with People First and the governor's advisors regarding road building, but he had to maintain the final say, as he was the expert in the area. Concerning sewage, water, and electricity, he guaranteed that all systems would be brought into compliance with the local codes.

Six months later

A fellow People First member, Jan Eberley, awakened Claire Muller shortly after dawn. Jan was quite upset. It seems that during the night, ENRC had removed all of the trees from a 3-acre parcel of land. Furthermore, when Jan and a group of People First representatives had gone out to the spot, the construction workers, none of whom were islanders, just laughed at them.

When Claire joined them at the site, the deforestation was complete. Mr. Hopkins was nowhere to be found. The new director of construction, Harmon Harper, had been hired only a few days earlier. "I was just following orders," he claimed.

18 months later

The resort had been completed for five months. Occupancy rates were high. So were the town noise levels.

The islanders were divided over their opinion of the resort. Some, allied with People First, went to the Governor's office. The Governor was unavailable. The Assistant to the Governor was unavailable. During the next month, 40 of the 275 islanders who worked at the resort were laid off. Some islanders tried to bring sanctions against ENRC but were unable to establish the legality of the contract. People First led a series of demonstrations outside the resort, causing a drop in the number of tourist visits.

Islanders found themselves bitterly divided. Some, appreciating the jobs, supported ENRC. Others, noting environmental degradation, opposed ENRC.

Case Questions

1. From a utilitarian perspective, how would you evaluate this case? How would you balance the benefits and harms?

2. Just for the sake of argument, make a case that People First, although it may be well intentioned, acted unethically.

3. Just for the sake of argument, make a case that ENRC, whatever its intentions, acted unethically.

4. What is your own perspective? How do you ethically evaluate this situation? Why?

Case Study—It's No Big Deal

Doug Cagney is the owner and manager of Dougie's Diner in Middlefork County. He has recently joined the Middlefork Restaurant Owner's Association (MROA). The group's bylaws include a section on protecting the environment. The MROA has been pressuring the Middlefork County government to start a recycling program for the county but has not been successful.

At the most recent meeting, the Association voted to voluntarily salvage all possible recyclable items at their respective establishments, such as aluminum soda cans, cardboard, Styrofoam containers, etc. The group planned to pay local college students to pick up the recyclables and haul them to a local reprocessing plant. The money that would be earned for the effort would go back to the Association to be used for scholarships for local students studying food service management at Middlefork Community College.

The clientele at Doug Cagney's diner was comprised of three main groups with different rush hours. The largest group contained hundreds of local high school students. There was a very busy two-hour lunch rush, and a second rush at 3 P.M. when school ended. The other busy times included breakfast for truckers who were always in a hurry, and early evening dinner specials that started at 5 P.M. for senior citizens. The diner, which was a weekday operation only, closed each evening promptly at 7 P.M. after a typical 13-hour day.

For several weeks after Doug joined the MROA, he valiantly tried to collect aluminum cans. He handed out flyers to all the students asking them to drop their cans in special receptacles. He spoke with truckers and senior citizens personally to ask for their assistance. He asked his employees to sift through the outside garbage for the aluminum. But the situation seemed hopeless. The only cans they were able to recover regularly were the ones that were served at the tables that the servers retrieved on their own. There was just not enough time in the day to salvage the cans when the customers would not assist. His employees refused to go through the garbage any longer.

After two months, Doug gave up. He didn't even bother recycling cardboard and Styrofoam any longer. He thought, "Why should I do this for everyone else when they won't even help themselves? Besides, how much harm can my little place be doing anyway?"

Case Questions

1. Does Doug have any responsibility to recycle in this situation? Why or why not?

2. What does a utilitarian analysis say Doug should do? Explain your answer.

3. What does a Kantian analysis say Doug should do? Explain your answer.

4. What do you think of Doug's explanation? Is he right in thinking that "his little place can't do much harm anyway?" Would Aristotle agree or disagree with you? Explain your answer.

5. If he chose to do something, Doug could concentrate primarily on his own restaurant's practices, or he could focus on broader attempts to change the public's habits through education, cooperative programs with other merchants and the county administration, etc. Is there any ethical reason to prefer one course of action to another? Whatever your answer, explain why you think so.

Case Study—Safety First

The City of Bridgeview, located on Long Island, directly on the Atlantic Ocean, has recently opened a public swimming area adjacent to a boating area that has been operational for five years. In order to ensure the safety of both the boaters and the swimmers, the City of Bridgeview Community Relations Director, Damon Bailey, has suggested that rules and regulations be instituted. He has drafted the following statement, which includes safety statistics, for his colleagues in Community Relations to consider:

1. *Persons boating must be licensed.*

    a. *People can only receive boating licenses after taking and passing a course on boating safety. The Office of Community Relations will offer such a course for a small fee. Licenses can also be obtained from outside concerns authorized by the Office of Community Relations; a list of such places will be made available.*

   b. *Persons boating without a license are subject to substantial fines.*

   c. *Allowing only licensed boaters on the water has been shown to decrease deaths and serious injuries by 78 percent.*

2. *Prohibit alcohol in boating and swimming areas.*

   a. *People who are impaired by alcohol do not make good swimmers.*

   b. *People who are impaired by alcohol do not make good boaters.*

   c. *The costs to the community involved with this measure could be substantial; costs could include loss of income if the location is used mainly for adult party purposes.*

   d. *Statistically, limiting alcoholic beverages in swimming and boating areas has shown to decrease deaths and serious injuries by 80 percent.*

3. *Ban swimming when rip currents are present.*

   a. *Rip currents are the most threatening natural hazard to be found along any coastline. The United States Lifesaving Association estimates that the annual number of deaths due to rip currents exceeds 100 deaths per year. Rip currents account for over 80 percent of rescues performed by surf beach lifeguards each year.*

   b. *If swimming when rip currents are present is not banned, the cost to the Community Relations Office will include increased death and injury liability insurance.*

   c. *Statistically, this measure has been shown to decrease deaths and serious injuries by 40 percent.*

4. *Do not allow any glass containers in swimming and boating areas.*

   a. *Broken glass causes libelous injuries.*

   b. *All beverages for sale should be in non-breakable containers. Presently there are some items sold that are in glass containers. These are sold because they are less expensive than the beverages in plastic containers (because the glass containers are recyclable and there is a substantial return for the recycled glass).*

   c. *Statistically, this measure has been shown to decrease all injuries by 30 percent.*

5. *Ban beach fires.*

   a. *Beach fires destroy the natural environment. Debris from beach fires is difficult to clean.*

   b. *Beach fires cause libelous injuries.*

    c. The Office of Community Relations will lose income if beach-goers choose other locations.

    d. Statistically, this measure has been shown to decrease death and serious injury by 65 percent.

6. *Prohibit scuba diving.*

    a. Scuba diving can cause serious medical conditions including inner ear barotraumas, Pulmonary barotraumas, Arterial gas embolism (AGE), and Decompression sickness ("the bends").

    b. The estimated annual death rate is 90 per year worldwide.

    c. Statistically, this measure has been shown to decrease death and serious injury by 88 percent.

A meeting was called to debate Mr. Bailey's suggestions. Heated discussion took place regarding whether or not to adopt any or all of the suggested measures.

Case Questions

1. What ethical issues are involved in this case? Explain your answer.

2. Which measures would you argue should be followed? Explain and defend your answer.

3. Going measure by measure, list the ethical arguments for adoption, or for not adopting, the proposed rule. Which type of ethical analysis are you using?

Ethics and Public Policy in the Hospitality and Tourism Industry

THIS CHAPTER EXAMINES the relationship between ethics and public policies that regulate the hospitality and tourism industry. Issues in this area can become very complex, and we can only scratch the surface here. However, the basic outlines of some of the major disagreements to be found in this arena can be laid out.

By "public policy" we mean laws and government regulations of business affairs. Public policy questions are inherently *political* in the sense that they concern what public officials should do. In a democratic society public policy questions are openly debated public issues that engage politicians, political parties, and legislatures.

Because public policy questions are political, they immediately get tangled up in issues that we do not think of as simple ethical issues. The phrase, "It's all politics," often means that the person saying it is so cynical about politics and the political process that he or she does not believe that normal rational perspectives can be applied. Instead, the person believes that self-interested, power-grabbing individuals or groups are bending things to their own interest. While this cynical viewpoint about politics may or may not be correct, it does not move political issues entirely beyond the reach of ethics. As with all human activities, political activities have ethical consequences, and therefore they can be judged ethically.

However, ethical issues that are also political issues are complicated by the fact that views on them inevitably are dependent on *ideology*. An ideology is a system of beliefs that are both factual and value-laden about the way the world works. Ideologies implicitly or explicitly answer basic questions about human nature (are we inherently selfish? benevolent? etc.), about the purpose of government (protect private property? reduce inequality? enforce majority will? protect individuals rights? etc.), about the "good society" (free? equal? just? conforming to the will of one's God or deity? etc.), and the like. Our ideologies, or outlooks, enormously influence how we see the world, and inevitably make us more sensitive to certain aspects of the world and perhaps less sensitive to others.

Thus, in many "political" arguments, because of ideological differences the two sides are talking past each other because they are discounting or not seeing "facts" to which the other side is appealing. Especially in politics, feelings can run very high, and sensitivity to the point of view or factual considerations of one's opponent is often missing. Therefore, it is important, when doing an ethical analysis of public policy debates, to exercise a certain degree of humility regarding ethical claims made for "your" side. This does not mean that morality is irrelevant in public policy discussions—different policies have very different motivations and consequences, and those differences are just as subject to ethical debate as any others.

Ideological views concerning governmental relations with business activities vary widely. At the one extreme is the perspective that there should be no governmental interference in the private affairs of businesses—an unregulated market should govern all aspects of business affairs. From this perspective, any government intrusion is immoral because it curtails freedom and inevitably leads to inefficiency and injustices. This ideology is often labeled "individualistic," with individuals and businesses allowed to acquire as much as possible free from government restraint or control.

In an earlier chapter, we noted the argument by Milton Friedman that businesses have no obligation of any sort beyond the obligation to make as much money as possible, just as long as they live within the basic "rules of the game" set up by society. Friedman believes that there should be few rules regulating business, other than certain basic ones enforcing contracts and preventing monopolistic or deceptive or unfair business practices. However, the real question is, "How far can the government go in setting up the rules of the game?" Even Friedman does not argue that there should not be any rules; only that rules should be minimal. Others may see a greater need for governmentally enforceable rules on a wider front, if they believe that corporate behavior will not likely achieve socially desired ends simply on a voluntary basis.

At the opposite extreme, socialist ideology argues that economic activities should be run and controlled by the government, because this is the only way such basic values as fairness and general equality can be protected from private plundering entities like large corporations. The private market is seen as a mechanism whereby the rich and powerful control and take advantage of those with less wealth. Freedom is conceived as "freedom from hunger," "freedom from insecurity and deprivation," etc., rather than freedom from societal ties and obligations.

Between the extremes of unregulated "pure" capitalism and socialism is the ideology of a "mixed economy"—a capitalist market economy that is primarily run by private enterprise, but with more or less extensive governmental intervention into that economy to protect public interests. Virtually all advanced industrial capitalist economies are of the "mixed" variety, including that of the United States. There are considerable differences between nations, with the United States having one of the less regulated economies while many European (especially Scandinavian) economies are considerably more regulated.

Within society, different groups with varying interests and ideologies tend to take opposite attitudes toward government regulation of business for "extraneous" (i.e., non-business) purposes. Groups such as environmental groups, women's rights groups, civil rights groups, organized labor, consumer protection groups, and others tend to favor government regulation of business activities to protect the various interests that they represent. They lobby government for environmental protection laws, laws banning discrimination against women or minorities, minimum wage laws, occupational safety, consumer protection and "truth-in-advertising", etc., laws that require businesses to adhere to certain standards.

On the other hand, industry and business organizations tend to oppose most regulations over business conduct, or at least those that cost money or restrict a company's freedom of action. While certain minimal regulations may be acceptable, industry and business groups in general feel that governmental regulation is unneeded, unduly cumbersome, expensive, and highly inefficient. They lobby government against any new regulations, or against expansion of existing regulations. The general outlook put forward by these groups is that businesses will be able to do much more for society if they are left to themselves to pursue profit-making ways to serve the public. Let's look at an example that we can analyze at a later point.

Case Study—The Public Exposure Debate

A coalition of organizations has been operating in the state of Wisconsin for quite some time. It is composed of consumer groups, labor unions, women's organizations, environmental groups, civil rights groups, activist student groups, gay rights groups, some religiously based social action groups, and low income community organizing groups. It is known as the Wisconsin Coalition for Progressive Action, or WCPA. WCPA has pursued an active agenda in the state for the past eight years, organizing constituencies and lobbying the state legislature to pass a number of bills, including ones to provide healthcare for all children in the state, to tighten the environmental regulatory process for new building developments, to ban state contracts with companies found guilty more than once of violating anti-discrimination employment laws, and to require businesses doing business with the state to remain neutral in the event its employees wish to form a labor union. It has been moderately successful, winning at least partial victories in a number of these campaigns.

WCPA has just unveiled a new campaign. Under the slogan, "All Business is the People's Business," it is pushing for a law requiring all businesses registered in the state with more than five employees to fill out yearly forms that will be filed with the state's commerce department. These forms are to be open to the public. They will list a number of things about the business that ordinarily might be kept private: the compensation of all top company officials making more than $100,000 per year; the number of employees, average wages paid to each category of company employee, how many of the company's employees receive health care insurance (and for those that do, what percentage of premiums the individual employee must pay), how many employees have a company-provided pension, any *business done by the company for the state or any other public entity within the state, and any violations of law the company has been found guilty of in the past ten years.*

WCPA spokesman, Milo Danver, issued a press release stating that companies are artificial creations that exist solely for the benefit of the people, therefore, the people have the right to know how these entities are behaving. Danver argues that this law would in no way restrict the freedom of companies in their behavior; it is simply a "sunshine law" requiring them to be transparent so that citizens can judge their overall impact on the community. Those who "external-ize" various obligations to the public, such as health care costs, costs of maintaining people in their old age (pensions), or who pay wages so low that their employees qualify for food stamps and other forms of public assistance, should be exposed for what they are doing. In that way, citizens (both as participants in public policy formation and as consumers) can decide in an intelligent and informed manner how they wish to relate to companies. Danver argues that this bill, if passed into law, would reward beneficial companies that raise living standards, provide health care insurance and pensions, and the like. The only ones it would punish, he claims are the "bad apples" among businesses that drag down living standards in the community, not the many businesses who abide by standards making their employ-ment practices beneficial to society as a whole.

Oliver Standifant, the spokesperson for the Wisconsin Food, Beverage and Entertainment Association (WFBEA), immediately sent out an "ALARM MEMO" to all the members of his association. Portions of Mr. Standifant's memo follow:

"The misguided idealists are at it again! We have just received word that they will be lobbying for a drastic change in state law that would have horrible consequences for every member of this association, not to mention the general public.

[At this point, the memo relates the details of the pro-posed law.]

This fundamental attack on our free enterprise system would harm the very people it is supposedly trying to help. If businesses can't set wages according to what the market dic-tates as fair and just compensation, but instead has to satisfy government bureaucrats and socialist-minded do-gooders, many businesses will be forced to go out of business. Effi-ciency will suffer enormously.

We also know that any bill like this will drive businesses away from our state. No one wants to invest and operate in a state that would treat its business citizens in such a hostile *manner. I can think of no other measure that does a better job of destroying job creation in our state.*

Each and every one of you will no longer be able to run your business as you see fit. Jobs will be lost by the tens of thousands. Those who were earning an entry-level wage will be left with no job and no wage at all.

The clammy hand of government bureaucracy is threatening us as never before. You must all contact your legislators to stop this proposed "bill" immediately.

In addition, we will need to double our "political fund" assessment of each association member, so that we can increase our ability to elect legislators who understand the needs of businesses in our industry. I will be calling an emergency meeting of our executive committee with the aim of instituting an immediate doubling of our political fund assessment, to fight this insidious attack upon us."

Milo Danver obtained a copy of this memo, and circulated it to all of the members of the WCPA coalition. In a letter accompanying the memo, Danver made the following assertions:

(1). *Absolutely no "dictating" of wages, healthcare coverage, pension coverage, or anything else is contained in the proposal.*

(2) *Transparency and accountability to the public is the real issue here, not an attack on the private enterprise economic system.*

(3) *There would be no loss of jobs if this bill were to pass, but there may be a number of embarrassed businesses that would improve the wages and/or healthcare coverage and/or pension coverage of their employees.*

(5) *The constituency of the organizations making up this coalition would benefit enormously if the law were passed, because the "underdog" and the "have-nots" would have a basis to expose mistreatment and a way to appeal to the public for policies ensuring better treatment.*

(6) *The WCPA feels that the ferocious counter-attack of the WFBEA means that political efforts will have to be increased greatly in the coming year, so that the "power of the people" is able to counter the "power of the moneyed interests" in their attempt to sway legislators.*

Case Commentary

If we attempt to analyze this case from an ethical perspective, it immediately becomes clear how "ideological" and "political" the case is. No ethical analysis is possible until a number of factual issues are cleared up, and these "factual issues" are deeply embedded in ideological viewpoints. In this text, we have no intention of reviewing different political ideologies and pronouncing one "correct" and another "wrong." But we can show how dependent our ethical conclusions are on our beliefs about factual matters, as well as how "ideological" our factual beliefs actually are.

In this case, there are a number of highly disputed assertions about what the "facts" are. Is it really true that this measure will have no harmful consequences in terms of the state's "business climate" and its ability to attract and retain businesses? If so, aren't there a lot of reasons for supporting the proposed legislation? Alternatively, is it really true that this legislation would distort the workings of the market in a way that impedes business efficiency and leads to increased unemployment? If so, isn't that a reason to strongly oppose this legislation? Is this an assault on private enterprise that will likely lead to ever more government meddling and an end to a vibrant economy? If true, this is a reason to oppose the measure. Or, is it a noble attempt to force private corporations to deal honestly and openly with the public citizens upon whom it depends for so much, simply by being transparent in its behavior? If true, this is a reason to support the proposed measure.

We could continue to multiply the "facts" that are strongly believed by proponents on each side, to show how each would likely sway our ethical judgment about what is the best stance to take on the proposed legislation. But we stop here, simply to note that these factual beliefs, bolstered by (and in many ways, dependent upon) an ideological outlook, can make all the difference in how one ethically sees matters of public policy such as this.

Mr. Danver and most of those who lead the organizations in his coalition sincerely believe that many (not all) corporations receive all sorts of "corporate welfare" (tax abatements, provision of public utilities, social welfare supports for low wage employees, favorable zoning and other treatment, etc.) from the public without providing equal value in return. They believe that strong governmental regulation of the market is absolutely necessary to ensure beneficial and fair treatment of individuals, especially those who are poorer or who are from vulnerable populations such as minorities or immigrants or women, etc. They believe that corporate entities, left to themselves, will "rip off" those more vulnerable and despoil the environment if they are not *required* (with sanctions backing up the requirements) to not do so—not because the individuals running those corporations are "bad" or "evil" but simply because the market rewards only profit-making, not ethical behavior. They also believe that governmental regulation of the sort envisioned by this measure will have no negative "unintended consequences" of any great importance.

Mr. Standifant and most of those who lead the businesses in his association sincerely believe that corporations are the productive element in the economy—the lynchpin that creates all the wealth that all citizens enjoy. They believe that corporations, far from receiving unduly favorable treatment, are often besieged from all sides by those trying to squeeze ever more out of the "goose that lays the golden egg." They believe that the business environment is already hard enough, and that further government intrusion into business matters is bound to wipe out a lot of productive businesses. They believe that a "free market," unfettered from government or other constraints, produces the best possible outcome to a society. They believe that most (although not all) businesses are run ethically, and that only minimal oversight is needed to ensure ethical behavior. For the most part, the market will "weed out" those that do not adhere to basic ethical standards.

Simply by looking at these contrasting beliefs, one can see that a utilitarian analysis, for example would arrive at diametrically opposed conclusions, depending on which of the two ideological worldviews the analyst adhered to. Using the same ethical perspective, but holding different factual beliefs, two utilitarians could easily end up on opposite sides of the issue. The same is true for a Kantian—who would be violating the categorical imperative if the measure does, or does not, pass thanks to the strenuous efforts of the proponents on one side or the other? A Kantian of one ideological worldview may see violation of the humanity of others (i.e., a violation of the categorical imperative) on one side or the other, depending on which set of facts he or she believed to be true. The same is true for a follower of justice ethics—which side is likely to lead to greater injustices? It all depends on the facts. And a "virtue ethicist" who is judging the character of Mr. Danver and Mr. Standifant would also have to sort out these ideological "factual" issues before making a good judgment of character.

The point of this is not to argue that ethical judgments about political matters are impossible, but rather to point out how important it is to establish what is factually true if we are to arrive at an agreed upon ethical judgment. And that becomes hard to do regarding political matters if we have different ideological outlooks that make us see a different set of "facts" in the world.

One thing to note is that here, as is often the case, each side seems to ideologically view the world as if what is best for *its own members* is also what's best for *society as a whole*. The private interests of each side's constituents are seen as identical to, or virtually identical to, the public interest. This is a very common tendency. That fact alone should warn us to carefully examine our own perspectives and look for biases toward seeing our own self-interest as always what's best for others. It is very hard to notice these biases, but we all should make the effort.

Minority viewpoints within the organizations on both sides are also possible, and perhaps even likely. For example, certain organizations that might normally operate within Mr. Danver's coalition may not join it on this particular issue, because they consider the legislation "going too far," unduly intrusive into the private affairs of businesses, unlikely to achieve its goals of aiding workers' wages and treatment, or other reasons. The leaders of a few businesses within Mr. Standifant's association might find the proposed legislation entirely unobjectionable because they are proud of their practices and would be happy to expose them to public scrutiny, while they consider some of their competitors "bottom feeders" taking unfair competitive advantage by substandard employment practices whose poor records they would be happy to see exposed. So, the interest groups that are mentioned in the case would probably not be unanimous in the stance that they took, but we believe the predominant sentiment would divide along the lines sketched out in the case.

For associations of businesses within the hospitality and tourism industries, the question regarding what stance to take toward various public policy issues often becomes: what is the most enlightened self-interest position to take? That is, which policy is likely to lead to the most beneficial consequences for the industry in the long run? They must determine what is the long run, and how to best calculate results over that period of time. When associations do this, they are clearly applying a utilitarian ethic, looking for the greatest benefits for the greatest number in the industry. However, if they take only an industry standpoint, they are simply acting as an interest group, not as a guardian of what will necessarily lead to the greatest good for the greatest number in society as a whole. Therefore, from the standpoint of society as a whole, their position must be measured in terms of its impact on everyone. If it still measures up as best, it is the ethical position, from a utilitarian perspective. Of course, justice and rights considerations may enter into the calculations also, if the particular issue being considered involves questions of rights and fairness.

Because public policies affect us all in major ways, it is important to apply an ethical perspective to them, hard though that may be. The difficult thing is to get to enough common ground in terms of political ideology to be able to make sound and widely acceptable judgments.

Case Study—A Fair Price to Pay

Christopher Hopkins is the State Representative from Louisiana, which is one of the states without a minimum wage law. This has not been an issue in the past as the federal minimum wage laws cover most workers.

Recently, a group of activists began advocating for the passage of a Louisiana minimum wage law. To complicate the issue, they want the state law to be sixty-five cents per hour higher than the federal government requires.

The Louisiana Food, Beverage & Entertainment Association (FBEA) has made it quite clear to Mr. Hopkins that they are against the passage of a state law. They believe that such a law will cut into profits so drastically that many small businesses will have to close and that even larger businesses will undoubtedly suffer.

The activist group, The People's Wage Society (TPWS) disagrees. They have statistics showing that businesses will not be so drastically affected. They also show how a person living in Louisiana, earning the minimum wage, could not possibly support a family of even 2 people. It would be hard enough to support one person, they vehemently argue.

Mr. Hopkins is conflicted. He is up for reelection in six months. The FBEA has donated quite a bit of money to his campaigns in the past. He has rarely had a disagreement with them. However, he can certainly see the points being made by TPWS. He must decide sometime in the next week because his constituents will be asking him questions while he is out campaigning for reelection.

Case Questions

1. Which side should Mr. Hopkins support? Explain your answer.

2. Formulate the fundamental principle on which each side would base its moral argument.

3. Would your decision depend on factual matters or moral conviction? Explain your answer.

4. Can political issues like this be based on moral premises? Explain your answer.

Case Study—Second-Hand Rose

Neptune County passed an anti-smoking ordinance in 1993. Three years later, the County Office on Law interpreted it to allow smoking in all bars while restricting smoking in restaurants to separate rooms. Presently, there are seventy eating and drinking establishments countywide that allow smoking. The number of places that allow smoking appears to be growing instead of diminishing.

Rose Manson had been a bartender for 12 years when she decided that working around second-hand smoke was hurting her lungs. She left Orly's Bar and Grille in Neptune County in 2004 under very friendly circumstances. She jokingly promised to return to work for Orly when he banned smoking at the bar.

Rose decided that she was going to assist the no-smoking effort in Neptune County. She wanted to help close the loophole that allowed a health hazard, such as smoking, to exist in separate restaurant dining rooms and in bars. She attended County Council meetings and lobbied with other concerned citizens. Three of five council members signed a pledge saying they would introduce or support legislation that made workplaces and public places completely smoke-free. Strangely, Mr. James Gladhand, the councilman who was most supportive and outspoken about the county's law to prevent tobacco sales to those under 18, would not sign onto the smoke-free effort.

Rose was disturbed about Mr. Gladhand's lack of support. She felt that if she could get his support, then they could not possibly lose. She delved into his background, trying to find common ground for discussion. While researching, she looked into his local business interests. She discovered that he was a silent partner in two of the neighborhood bars where smoking was presently permitted.

While she was at it, Rose looked into another local politician she thought she could get help from, Victor Shadder. Mr. Shadder had long been a proponent of the smoking ban. During her research, Rose discovered that Mr. Shadder received very large sums of money for his campaigns from smoking opponents.

Case Questions

1. What are the major arguments that support Mr. Gladhand's position? Explain your answer.

2. What are the major arguments that support Rose's position? Explain your answer.

3. In light of your answers to questions 1 and 2, are there any factual issues that need to be clarified to help settle the question of whose position has a better ethical justification?

Case Study—Fishy Facts: The Good, the Bad, and the Ugly

You decide. The following are facts about fish as a food product.

GOOD	BAD	UGLY
Low in saturated fat	Leading route of exposure to methyl mercury	Mercury impairs fetal brain development
High in protein	Women who eat fish more 3+ times per week have mercury levels that are 7X higher than women who eat no fish	The Environmental Protection Agency (EPA) estimates one in six US babies born yearly with unsafe methyl mercury blood level
Excellent source of omega-3 fatty acids	Fish are vulnerable because, in water, toxic substances can reach higher levels because of the longer food chains	Top predatory fish, like tuna, can have extremely high levels of mercury—much higher than the water level it is swimming in
Omega 3 FAs reduce blood pressure and build healthy brains in children	The placenta can not filter out methyl mercury	Methyl mercury halts cell division in the fetal brain

Information from Fishy Facts, Sandra Steingraber, "How mercury-tainted tuna damages fetal brains," In these Times, Jan, 2005, pg 16-17, 29.

Case Questions

1. Should factory emissions of methyl mercury into the environment be limited? If so, what would be the cut-off point for the cost?

2. How do we balance the cost to the industry against the brain damage? Should there be a "trade off" or should emissions be cut drastically *no matter what the cost*?

3. Apply utilitarianism, Kantian duty ethics, and Rawlsian justice ethics to questions 1 and 2 above.

4. Should women eating in restaurants be warned about eating fish, especially fish at the top of the food chain, such as tuna and swordfish? If so, who is responsible for doing the warning and why?

🔍 Case Study—Loyal Beyond the Letter of the Law ———————

A recent study by Victuals Insurance, an insurance company that specializes in insuring restaurants, found that slips, trips, and falls by patrons are the most common general liability insurance claims filed by full service restaurants. Furthermore, slips, trips and falls represent about twenty-seven percent of workers' compensation claims. The Victuals Company mailed an information notice to its clients suggesting that an extra focus on safe flooring, adequate lighting, and quick clean up of spills could help operators cut insurance costs.

The notice from Victuals intrigued Edna Beckman, who owns Variety Delicatessen and Restaurant in Novo City. She followed all of the advice: she had the flooring changed (at great cost), she had the lighting upgraded (at further cost), and she fervently monitored any spills including rain, snow, and mud that could get tracked in when the weather was poor.

Within two years time, she noticed a definite drop in insurance claims. She compared claim costs five years ago to the cost of the previous year and she was delighted. Furthermore, her insurance premium was lowered.

Two weeks after doing her personal comparative study, Crenshaw, one of Edna's most loyal chefs fell in the kitchen. He suffered severe back strain and was told that he needed complete bed rest. Six months later, Workers' Compensation insurance and sick days had dried up for Crenshaw. He started using up his accrued vacation. His back was still severely strained. Nine months later, Crenshaw was still unable to return to work as a chef. However, Edna thought she might utilize his talents in the office. She spoke to Crenshaw and they agreed that he would come in two mornings per week to do some bookwork. Edna continued to pay Crenshaw his full salary.

Later that month Edna's lawyer and business partner, Frank Malloy, came by to discuss an upcoming audit. When he saw that Edna was giving Crenshaw his full salary, he became angry and shouted, "Why are we paying him? And, why are we paying him full salary? We are not required by law to pay him. Why do you think we have laws governing these types of issues?"

Case Questions

1. What should Edna do? Explain your answer and base it on at least one of the theories we have studied.

2. Explain Malloy's point of view. What is his reasoning?

3. Develop a policy for handling situations of this type that you feel is fair to all concerned. Is this policy based on any of the ethical theories we have studied?

🔍 Case Study—Menu Management ———————————————————

Adrian is the cashier at the Hi Ho Burger Shop. The small boutique restaurant specializes in all different types of burgers including vegetarian burgers. This evening Stephanie, one of Adrian's friends who is a vegetarian, came into the restaurant and ordered the Whoop-de-do, which is a soy burger.

Within one minute of Stephanie's first bite, she began choking. Adrian, who is trained in first aid, jumped up and immediately began to slap Stephanie on her back. But Stephanie fought her off and instead, reached into her purse and pulled out a needle, which later turned out to be a strong antihistamine. As soon as she had started coughing, Stephanie realized that the burger must contain nuts; she is severely allergic to nuts.

Stephanie settled down and left shortly afterwards. She promised to see her doctor first thing in the morning.

The next day Adrian spoke to her boss Leonard about the matter. She suggested to Leonard that the menu should contain labels of all the ingredients that are used so that there are no more incidents. She told Leonard how scared she was for her good friend Stephanie.

Leonard listened politely but then he explained why he would not list the ingredients. He made it clear that it is the customer's responsibility to ask if certain ingredients are used in a menu item. He added, "Customers know when they have problems. If we start with nuts, it will never stop. Next it will be milk, then eggs. Then people will want to know how many calories. I won't have it."

Case Questions

1. Whose point of view do you agree with in this case? Explain your answer.

2. Which theorist would agree with your rationalization? Explain your answer.

Index

A

Adelphia, 7
affirmative action, 47–48
Aquinas, St. Thomas, 52
Arby's, 4
Aristotle, 49–52, 54, 61, 113

B

Bentham, Jeremy, 18–19, 20
bribery, 56–63
business ethics, 3–15
    cynical view of, 3–4
    financial benefits of,
      10–11
business responsibilities, 7

C

carelessness, 12
Carroll, Archie B., 7
categorical imperative, 26–28,
    59, 75, 87–88, 99–100,
    111–112
chain of command, 12–13
collective guilt, 46–47
consequences, 17, 25, 27, 32,
    57–58, 74, 87, 99
cost-benefit analyses, 18–19

D

deontology, 25, 74–75
difference principle, 42–44
duty, 5, 25, 26, 31–32
DWG Corporation, 4

E

egalitarians, 38
employment-at-will doctrine,
    6
Enron, 7, 55
equal liberty, 41, 42, 60, 112
equality, 37–38
ethical custom, 4–5
ethics
    and feelings, 14
    and law, 2, 5–7, 86–89

    and morality, 1
    schools of thought, 14

F

fair equality of opportunity,
    42, 44
freedom, 20, 33
Friedman, Milton, 4–5, 33, 140

G

golden mean, 50–51
golden rule, 27
greatest good, 17, 18, 57–58,
    98–99

H

happiness, 18, 19–20, 22, 23
Hitler, Adolf, 3
human rights, 20

I

ignorance, 12

J

justice, 1, 20, 21
    compensatory, 47–48
    distributive, 37–39
    retributive, 46–47
justice ethics, 37–48, 60–61, 76,
    88–89, 100–101, 112–113,
    131, 133, 145

K

Kantian ethics, 25–35, 58–60,
    74–75, 87–88, 99–100,
    111–112, 130, 132–133, 145
    criticisms of, 30

L

libertarianism, 32–34
loyal agent, 5

M

Marx, Karl, 39
Michales, Alex, 5
Mill, John Stuart, 19–20
mitigating circumstances,
    12–13
moral responsibility, 12–13
moral upbringing, 13
moral virtues, 50–52

N

Nelson, Katherine, 10

O

Olympic Games, 7
original position, 40–41, 42,
    44, 76
    criticisms of, 45

P

pain, 18–19
pleasure, 18–19, 23
Posner, Victor, 4
prisoner's dilemma, 8–10
private morality, 2–3

R

Rawls, John, 39–45, 60–61,
    75–76, 112–113
    criticisms of, 45
    and utilitarianism, 42
reason, 26, 27, 50
religion, 3, 14, 53, 60–61
rights, 1–2, 21
    and Kant, 28–30, 32, 34
    negative, 29–30, 32, 34
    positive, 29, 32, 34

S

slavery, 5–6, 20–21
social responsibility, 10–11

T

Treviño, Linda, 10

U

Uniform Deceptive Trade
   Practices Act, 86
utilitarianism, 17–24, 57–58,
   74, 87, 98–99, 110–111, 130,
   132, 145, 146
      act, 21–22, 57–58, 99

and Kant, 25–26, 30
and Rawls, 42–43
   rule, 21–22, 58, 99
utility, 17

V

veil of ignorance, 40–41, 44,
   60, 76, 88, 100, 112, 113
   criticisms of, 45
Velasquez, Manuel, 13
virtue ethics, 49–54, 76–77, 89,
   100, 113, 131, 133, 145

criticisms of, 52–53
and human nature, 52
and moral principles,
   51–52
and multiculturalism,
   52–53
and Rawls, 54
and social institutions,
   54

W

WorldCom, 7, 55